Performance versus Results

SUNY Series, The Philosophy of Education
Philip L. Smith, Editor

Performance versus Results

*A Critique of Values
in Contemporary Sport*

J O H N   H.   G I B S O N

STATE UNIVERSITY OF NEW YORK PRESS

Published by
State University of New York Press, Albany

© 1993 State University of New York

For information, address State University of New York
Press, State University Plaza, Albany, N.Y., 12246

Production by Diane Ganeles
Marketing by Bernadette LaManna

Library of Congress Cataloging-in-Publication Data
Gibson, John H., 1956-
    Performance versus results : a critique of values in contemporary
sport / John H. Gibson.
        p.   cm. — (SUNY series, the philosophy of education)
    Includes bibliographical references (p.   ) and index.
    ISBN 0-7914-1353-5 (cloth : alk. paper). — ISBN 0-7914-1354-3
(pbk. : alk. paper)
    1. Sports—Moral and ethical aspects.   2. Sportsmanship.
3. Sports—Social aspects.   4. Sports—Philosophy.   I. Title.
II. Title: Performance versus results.   III. Series: SUNY series in
philosophy of education.
GV706.3.G53   1993
175—dc20   92-8117
                                                                        CIP

10   9   8   7   6   5   4   3   2   1

TO SUSAN AND RYAN
&
FOR MY MOTHER AND FATHER

"You've got no feeling for the game at all, man. You'll win, but it'll just be numbers on the scoreboard. Numbers, that's all you care about . . . But that's not enough for me."

—Peter Gent, *North Dallas Forty*

Contents

Acknowledgments

I wish to express my sincere thanks to the teachers and other learned souls who have helped to frame the issues, pose the questions, and provoke me to look for answers over my years of formal and less formal study at: St. Luke's College, Marshall University, and The Ohio State University.

I am particularly grateful to Professor Sy Kleinman for holding open the window in academia at OSU that allowed me to pursue my interests, and at the same time providing psychic shelter from the slings and arrows of outrageous and uncomprehending souls. I am grateful to Professor Melvin L. Adelman for the hours he generously spent in working to correct my innumerable technical errors in the previous drafts of this document. Acknowledgment and enormous thanks are due to Professor Philip Smith: acknowledgment as the philosophical father of much of this project; and thanks for the friendship and strength which helped me to follow through on this task. Thanks are also due to Julia Good for technical editing and Susan Gibson for manuscript preparation.

Cheers mates.

Introduction

This study examines the problem of values in contemporary sport and offers an alternative conception of sport and its relationship to values.

Today much of sport exists under a value system that recognizes the objectivity of the scoreboard as the only true assessment of worth, and denies the value of the subjective, experiential, and personal dimensions of sport. The concomitant emphasis on winning has come at the expense of the relationship of the athlete to his craft. This problem exists to a greater or lesser extent at all levels of sport, and can be detected from little leagues and intramurals to professional leagues and internationals.

North Atlantic culture, in general, has an emphasis on "objectivity" which has had an effect on the development of its system of values. The result is that the powerful and rich tend to be viewed as inspirational personifications of the good, and often power is seen, in the most vulgar sense, as virtue.

Graphic examples of this value system can sadly be found in European professional soccer. For example, Tottenham Hotspurs, of London, England, met CF Barcelona of Barcelona, Spain, in the semi-final of the 1982 European Cup Winners Cup. The second and deciding leg was played in Barcelona in front of a packed and hysterical crowd. The Spanish team won and the crowd was ecstatic with joy, but the behavior of the Barcelona players was so violent over both legs of the tie that UEFA fined the victorious Spanish team for bringing the game into disrepute. Barcelona went on to win the competition playing equally as disreputably in the final. The Barcelona supporters were delighted that their team had won a major European soccer trophy but seemed incapable of seeing that the method by which the victory was achieved made it worthless. The great name of

1

CF Barcelona, a club steeped in history and tradition, was discredited, along with the reputation of Spanish soccer as a whole, in the eyes of the rest of the soccer community. Moreover, the game of soccer itself was once again discredited in the eyes of the community at large.[1]

This is an all too common example of the values of contemporary society. The victory is seen as being more important than the way in which it is achieved. Quality of performance is secondary to the result, and the values of the game are eclipsed by the cash value of winning.

Previous works in sport philosophy that have addressed the problems of values in the realm of sport have not dealt directly with the issue of valuing results over performance. They have tended either to apply various ethical theories to sport, without any real feeling for the value of sport,[2] or alternatively, where the value of sport is examined, it is done without consideration of the social context. The values of sport are taken to be self-generating or as existing independently of cultural values as a whole. Both of these types of analysis of sport tend to be reductionist or formalist in nature, mirroring the approaches and positions of formalist and reductionist philosophers as a whole.[3]

The various existential positions that have been articulated offer an alternative to both of these trends in sport philosophy. However, these tend to focus on the personal nature of sport experience at the expense of isolation from the social setting.[4] On one extreme the traditional philosophical lines are redrawn in sport, and on the other extreme, the position becomes almost mystical.[5]

The problem this study faces can be characterized in the same way. In providing a critique of contemporary sport I do not wish to remain too close to traditional sport philosophy, otherwise this work will become just another reworking of the previous efforts. On the other hand, I do not wish to depart too radically from the tradition of sport philosophy or I will be accused of changing the subject or leaving the field. In this study I will argue for a position that relates the existential nature of the individual in sport to the political and social world. I am offering a cultural criticism[6] that explains the development of values in contemporary sport, and illustrates an existential basis for alternative values in sport. The existential position outlined is quite capable of surviving in the contemporary cultural climate as well as providing the basis of communal relationships. It is the key to escaping from the situation where results are valued over performance.

It is my contention that the root of the contemporary emphasis on results lies in the explosion of rationality and objectivity that characterizes the Enlightenment. The power and achievement of the scientific method led to objectivity being seen as one of the hallmarks of truth. The criteria of reason and objectivity have been applied in a host of inappropriate situations and contexts ever since. Instrumental values dominate contemporary society and the value of things in themselves has become an outdated concept.

In an attempt to explain the creeping malaise within our values, this study will examine the major critiques of contemporary society in the work of Friedrich Nietzsche, Karl Marx, Johan Huizinga, Christopher Lasch, Alasdair MacIntyre, and Jurgen Habermas. Then an alternative basis for values in contemporary sport will be developed from the work of Nietzsche, MacIntyre, Habermas, Richard Rorty, and Drew Hyland.

MacIntyre seeks to foster a return to "something like" the virtues according to Aristotle, and outlines the basis for the social and personal elements that would support such a return.[7] I will attempt to show that the role of "something like" the virtues according to Aristotle in MacIntyre's work can be replaced by "something like" Nietzschean perspectivism, in the form of Hyland's stance of responsive openness, Rorty's "willingness to talk," and the Socratic virtue of dialogue.[8] At the same time, MacIntyre's social and personal framework can be retained and provides a basis for valuing sport in itself. Nietzsche claimed that art was the true medium for understanding human existence, and to this end the athlete can be seen as a performing artist, rather than a subject of quantification and objectification. The substitution of dialogue and openness of Aristotle is based on the belief that our best chance of acting properly lies in a willingness to examine our alternatives and not in our allegiance to some external iron law. From such an open stance our values in sport could emphasize the quality of performance, and value could be acknowledged by standards other than instrumental efficacy. Then the athletes' craft could provide a humanizing theme for their lives.

The Narrative

This work is divided into two parts, each comprised of three chapters. Part one constitutes an examination of the values in contemporary sport and society.

The initial chapter examines the philosophical earthquake of the Enlightenment followed by an exploration of the development of contemporary values. This is the cultural backdrop against which contemporary sport has emerged.

Chapter 2 deals specifically with the consequences of the post-Enlightenment value system on contemporary sport. The emergence of modern sport is examined, its characteristics discussed, and a distinction is made between modern sport forms and commodified sport. Commodified sport is a capitalistic rationalization of sport in which the sport is administrated in such a way as to maximize profits and capital accumulation. Thus, sport becomes just another means to the ends of capitalism and is no longer an area of intrinsic value. The Marxist critique of commodified sport is examined along with the Communist countries' views of contemporary sport and their failings to provide a humanizing alternative to the abuses of commodification. The chapter concludes with Lasch's critique of Huizinga, when he claims that sport has become commodified because we no longer take it seriously.

The final chapter in this section examines James Keating's claim that athletic excellence resides in winning. This assertion is taken as a quintessential contemporary statement of values, an axiom for today.[9] It is necessary, for the nature of this work, that Keating's position be overcome, otherwise there can be no escape from a world that values results over performance, for this is just what he is arguing. The case against Keating's position is developed from Hyland's concept of the stance of responsive openness.

The second part of the work explores the possibilities for developing a basis for values in sport offered by contemporary thinkers of the Nietzschean genre.

Chapter 4 analyzes the work of MacIntyre and his construction of a framework of practice, narrative unity, and tradition by which he claims that both the virtues and community can be preserved. My claim is that MacIntyre's social framework can support a view of sport that escapes the valuation of results over performance. He offers the choice between Nietzscheanism and Aristotelianism, a choice which he sees as being between a virtuous world and moral wasteland. According to MacIntyre's view, if we do not accept a form of Aristotelianism, then we are doomed to Nietzscheanism.

In the next chapter I argue that MacIntyre fails to convince us that his Aristotelianism is necessary or workable, or that the Nietzschean world is necessarily the horrendous one MacIntyre believes it must be. The Nietzschean world is the backdrop for the work of Habermas and Rorty, but they would not agree with MacIntyre's view. Nietzschean perspectivism forms the basis for the ungrounded philosophy of Rorty and Hyland's play stance. It is my contention that these can be substituted for MacIntyre's Aristotelian grounding, and his social structures of practice, narrative unity, and tradition, can still be kept. The basis becomes one of authentic communication instead of Greek metaphysics.

Chapter 6 applies the potentials opened to sport in a Nietzschean world. Both the horror and creativity of the "overman" are addressed, together with the resulting possibilities of sport as an art form, and the athlete as an artist. Finally, sport as a practice, in MacIntyre's sense, is explored. It is from the alternatives offered by these concepts that a new value system for sport can be created.

PART ONE

An Archaeology of Contemporary Sport

CHAPTER 1

The Problem of Values in Contemporary Society

The first task of this study is to trace the development of values in contemporary society. This will encompass a sweep from the birthplace of Western Civilization in ancient Greece, through the Enlightenment, to the present day. This trail leads directly to the values exhibited in contemporary sport which I wish to question. It is necessary to follow these developments so we might better understand what it is we are up against in contemporary culture, and why it has developed that way.

In this work, the Enlightenment is taken as the principle cataclysmic event that set Western culture on its route to contemporary values. The Enlightenment represents the ascendancy of reason over revelation. While the Reformation could be said to have given warning of the coming power and significance of the individual in society, it was still essentially a religious movement, albeit a religious reflection of growing individualism and materialism. The Reformation was concerned with religious freedom, we might say, while the Enlightenment came to represent freedom from religion and all other absolute authorities.

Ancient Greece Idealized

Ever since the enormous and heroic efforts of the Enlightenment released man from the chains of his organic past, setting in motion his metamorphosis into the liberal individual we recognize today, there has been a yearning in certain academic circles for the great days of ancient Greece. The work of many writers and philosophers even to this day articulate a somewhat romantic desire to return to, or at least revive, the era of man's greatest flowering.

9

Michael Harrington depicts George Wilhelm Friedrich Hegel as just such a scholar, and maintains that Hegel was trying to create a "modern society as organic as the Greece of his youthful imagination."[1] The desire to marry the ancient and organic with the modern and manufactured is a recurrent theme in many works. The belief that drives this desire is rooted in the notion that in ancient Greek society there was something that we lack, and are the lesser for it. MacIntyre suggests what we lack is the sense of the values, virtues, and purpose, or *telos*, that illuminated ancient Greek society.[2]

However, when the mythically idyllic existence in ancient Greece is examined it becomes apparent that the era so dotted upon is Hellenic only, and revolves solely around the city state of Athens. Furthermore, there was a price to pay for the harmonious and balanced development of man and the life of contemplating the Good, Beautiful, and Just, that was promoted there.[3] The price was slavery, and even death for non-citizens. Athenian democracy was extended to adult male citizens only. Individual freedom was not the major concern of this society; the primary function of the citizen was to serve the city. This society was organic and prescriptive with a high price to pay for tampering with established beliefs and practices. This form of impiety was the Athenian justification for executing Socrates and would have cost Aristotle as dearly if he had not chosen ". . . to save Athens from twice sinning against philosophy," and flee the city.

The idealized concept of ancient Athens sometimes clouds the true nature of her existence. Our contemporary concepts of democracy revolve around freedom and equality, whereas that of Athens was built on slavery and privilege. Even the citizens were servants of the city and existed under an aristocracy. The Greek Enlightenment is largely credited with bringing about the downfall of the ancient Greeks; is it true, too, of the Northern Europeans and their Enlightenment?[4]

The Enlightenment

When early Christianity developed its theological principles, and especially later in the Scholasticism of the Middle Ages, much was inherited and borrowed from Plato and Aristotle, notably in 'Aristotelianism' and the work of St. Thomas Aquinas. The universal truths that explained the world and man's place in it were enshrined in church law. This process underwrote the authority of virtually all ancient and medieval European society in the form of Scholasticism. Until the Enlightenment, Europe was a collection of organic, ascriptive societies, torn by war, ruled by royalties who reigned by God's will, and where the church was the broker of truth and power.[5]

The developments of the Renaissance led to a flowering of humanistic thought in the sixteenth century, epitomized by the tolerance and intellectual modesty found in the work of Michel de Montaigne. From this stance of virtual perspectivism, final absolute truth is not seen as an attainable goal of human reflection and study. The resulting ambiguity and plurality of views and beliefs, and the contradicting demands that they make on the individual, were all seen as part of the price of being human with no access to God's view.

However, the humanism of the sixteenth century was overtaken by rationalism in the seventeenth century. Stephen Toulmin describes this change as the move from the practical to the theoretical in philosophical thought. The oral traditions were replaced by the increasingly available written texts: formal logic supplanted rhetoric, the particular, concrete, local and timely, all gave way to the universal, general, abstract, and timeless.[6]

Toulmin traces the cause of this remarkable swing to the unsettled and shifting nature of Western Europe at this time. The conflicts of the Reformation coincided with a sustained attack on traditional cosmology. There grew out of this a great felt need for the re-creation of stability and hierarchy, something humanistic tolerance was less equipped to deliver than rationalist certitude.[7]

Thus, Toulmin takes the desire of seventeenth century thinkers to hold their quaking world together and forge a new framework for their existence, as the birth of modernity in the sciences. Toulmin also takes the sixteenth century Renaissance humanists as signaling the start of modernity in the humanities. It was the desire for certitude and stability that led the rationalists to gain hegemony over the humanistic view. This vital change paved the way for the emergence of the contemporary world where results, timeless and universal, are valued over performance, temporal and particular.

One of the major consequences of the Enlightenment was the overthrow of the absolute power of the church with the right of the individual to determine his own values. This process did not happen quickly, but was the result of generations of painful and difficult choices. What started as liberation under the banner of reason and science ended in rampant individualism and arbitrary value claims.

The crucial thing is that each person now had the potential to interpret the world for themselves. The Enlightenment produced individual freedom from the chains of the traditional interpretations of the universals by authorities. The power of individual reason became the liberating force of the age. One thinks readily of the precursor, in the Reformation of Martin Luther, freeing the Christian from papal infallibility and the reliance upon priests to interpret the Bible. Similarly the English, French, and American Revolutions were all fought in the name of individual freedom and liberty. Perhaps one of the most significant philosophical achievements was that of Rene Descartes. He created a method of inquiry open to use by all to free individuals from the pronouncements of others.

In response to Montaigne's claim that "unless some one thing is found of which we are completely certain, we can be certain about nothing," Descartes developed the *cogito*; the one thing of which he could be certain.[8]

Descartes' initial step was to doubt all that could not be demonstrated. This notion effectively demolished the ruined cloisters of scholasticism, as he rejected all existing knowledge. In the same way that old buildings are to be demolished before new ones are built, he cleared and leveled the intellectual landscape. Descartes doubted all except his own existence, which was proved to his satisfaction in the famous axiom, "I think, therefore I am." From this apparent solipsism Descartes devised a method for testing empirical information through the use of rational thought, a method by which a proposition could be affirmed as true if it passed tests of clarity and distinction. From this position Descartes sought to reconstruct the physical world, and in the process helped create scientific method as we know it today. In fact, the use of Descartes' method, with the individual as the central figure, led to the development of the contemporary western world.[9]

Rational thought and reason were the major tools of the Enlightenment, but they came to have narrow meanings and too broad an application. Simply put, rational came to mean the most efficient means to an end. Reason lost its root of reasonableness, fairness, and came to be synonymous with logic, and flowered poisonously as logical positivism.[10] Furthermore, the powerful conceptual weapon of reason was brought to bear frivolously, not just on agents of oppression, but on any part of society for which the individual did not care. Thus, all existing values and standards were brought into question and measured against the cold rod of reason, rationality, and efficiency.

It must be remembered that the Enlightenment did represent a legitimate liberation from oppressive and arbitrary authority. Contemporary western society was made possible by the struggles of the Enlightenment period, and as such we are all children of the Enlightenment. However, the problem created at this juncture was that the scientific method that grew out of the Enlightenment could not discover, detect, or create values. Mathematics, in the hands of

Newton, gave a degree of understanding to the universe but could not find God anywhere in it. The arbitrary rule of tyrants and false belief were quite rightly attacked and undermined, but pious men found themselves undermining the existence of God as well. Immanuel Kant suffered from this contradiction. He regarded the existence of God as paramount to man's political, social, and philosophical life. Yet his philosophical scholarship resulted in the systematic destruction of all traditional proofs of that existence.[11]

This was no malicious attempt to remove God. Kant was not happy with his position but it was not his by choice. The undermining of God appeared almost as a by-product of the process of the Enlightenment. Science successfully dealt with the world and its existence, with what "is", but no Enlightenment product could help with the realm of "ought", of values, now split from their traditional, irrational "proofs". No level of rational thought could convince that God is in his heaven, the soul immortal, and the will free. The consequence of this was shattering to Kant since he realized that those beliefs were the cornerstone of all moral values in the western world. Hegel also faced this issue, and posed the question of the Enlightenment's alternative to the displaced superstitions and prejudices. What was to replace all that had been destroyed?

Harrington claims that the alternative was the French Revolution. For Hegel the French Revolution, or "magnificent sunrise" as he called it, was to become excessively rational and destroy all the humane buffers between the individual and the state; an abstract society with no human mediation, but with radical individualism ripping community apart; a process that would lead to the terror itself. Hegel believed that with the overthrow of the absolute and universal truths, and the failing of political and social values, reason took refuge in private rights, and personal well-being became an end in itself.[12] The Enlightenment really had no alternatives. It was an escape "from", and not an escape "to".

Concepts of value now cut from the sacred and communal roots came to reside in personal reason, the basis for which was initially accepted as intuitive. However, subjective claims of this nature became discredited by the emerging power of sense data, objectified in scientific method. This new epistemological view, which John Locke championed, holds that all knowledge is empirical. At the end of this road lies logical positivism, which holds that "Truth" is attainable through scientific method.

Jean-Jacques Rousseau offered an opposing view, stressing the importance of feelings, art, and culture, and firing a resurgence in transcendentalism. However, both positivism and transcendentalism hold that an objective reality, "Truth", exists. For logical positivism it is the true empirical understanding of the material world. For transcendentalism there is more to Truth than scientific method can show.

The quest for truth eclipsed the quest for the good. Truth, it was claimed, can be known through rational thought, while good is merely a statement of preference. Thus, all values become instrumental, which is no value at all, in a moral sense. Despite the efforts of such great philosophers as Kant and Hegel, the Enlightenment failed to produce a feasible rational basis for moral action, or for standards of goodness and virtue. What the Enlightenment had done, in short, was to remove the hope that something universal and absolute (God, for example) was underwriting existence. The notion that there is such a certainty and order in the world is what Nietzsche called "metaphysical comfort". It was the loss of such comfort that was the price of the individual's freedom gained in the Enlightenment.

The Being, Becoming, Doing, and Having Ideal Cultural Types

An illuminating view of the consequences of the Enlightenment for contemporary culture can be gained using William Sadler's distinctions between Being, Becoming, Doing, and Having ideal cultural types.[13] Sadler identifies these four cultural types from history; they are by no means exhaustive, but are the most useful to this study of western cultural development. While no given culture is completely identical to the ideal cultural types described here, it is helpful to use them as abstract terms to describe and compare cultural values of the past and present. They can also be used to help present an account of how results came to be valued over performance.

The Being culture is typified by a primitive, highly traditional, and organic existence. The great time is held to have been in the past, and the present is only important as an extension of the glorious past. People in Being cultures tend to be fatalistic, dominated by the forces of the past and of nature. They show no desire to change their lot, rather they accept what happens to them as inevitable. The lives and values of the past are lived out in the present, with an emphasis on ritual and custom. The individual finds his own value as an expression of the will of the group in playing his allotted role within the demands of nature. The religious motif in Being cultures is not one of revelation or understanding but sacrifice, giving up one thing in order to attain something else.

In the Becoming culture the present is of the greatest importance. The past is thought of as gone, and the future as uncertain. Necessity and the forces of nature are respected, but nature is also seen as presenting possibilities and opportunities. Nature is not seen as dominant, but as a partner in life as the future unfolds. "In Aristotle's grand conception of this perspective, all of reality is moved by the dynamics of actualizing potentials."[14] The individual seeks self-development through cooperation rather than submission and obedience. The goal of life is taken to be the fulfillment of human potential. In a Becoming type culture, both the individual and society should strive for excellence. However, there are internal limits on what and how to achieve. The Delphic Oracle's directive to "know thyself", in this context means, "know your limits". In ancient Athens the worst sin was to fall into a state of *hubris*, the condition marked by overbearing pride, boastfulness, and arrogance. In other words, overstepping your mark.[15] In such a cultural context, competition might serve a useful purpose, that of driving competitors to higher levels of excellence, but not as a basis for distributing scarce resources.

The third cultural type is the Doing, in which the future is seen as more important than the present. The present is important but mainly as the gateway to the future, which is thought of as a better place. Nature is neither oppressive nor a partner, but a wealth of raw materials to be exploited. In ancient Athens man's limits were emphasized, and they feared overstepping them. But in the Doing culture limits are unknown, and the fear is of never reaching them. Normative activity in the Doing culture is doing, producing, getting things done. Hard work is valued, and production is held to be more important than preserving social relations, manners, customs or a concern for others' feelings. All of these considerations can be legitimately set aside if they threaten maximized production. Within a Doing culture people fear "not making it", and the struggle for success leads to an institutionalization of competition, not only as a valuable activity, but also as a system of justice. Competition no longer functions as an aid to maximizing human potential, as a way to reach higher levels of excellence, but as a way of striving for dominance. Winning becomes a virtue in itself.

The fourth cultural type, the Having, is marked by a shift in normative behavior from production to consumption. In a Doing culture what one does defines one's status, but in a Having culture what one owns defines one's status. The doer, or producer looks to the future for rewards; he defers gratification. Whereas, the haver, or consumer, looks for instant gratification of short term needs. In the

Having culture, nature is perceived not just as something to be used in production, but as property to be owned, consumed or "had". While normative behavior is consumption, the method of acquisition of the commodity is of no importance. Possession as a form of conspicuous consumption is taken as an indication of personal worth. There is no moral worth needed to buy anything. At least a culture built on production demanded achievement, some ability, but the culture of consumption admires huge appetites and great indulgences and nothing more.

While still existing in their own right, the four ideal cultural types outlined here also map out the flow of cultural development in the western world, from ancient Greece to contemporary America. Homeric Greece was a Being culture which changed through the Greek Enlightenment into a Becoming culture. When Greece gave way to Roman domination, and Rome subsequently collapsed into barbarism, Europe was returned to a Being culture. This cultural epoch was ended when the European Enlightenment once again developed Becoming cultures. This time the process set in motion did not stop at Becoming, but developed in the modern west into Doing type cultures. In contemporary western society, notably in the United States, we see cultures of Having. The cultural types of Doing and Having can be taken as direct cultural responses to a modern world where the basis for moral action has been eroded by a process that started nearly four hundred years ago.

From Character to Personality

The Enlightenment essentially attacked the concept and existence of universal absolute truth. The moral vacuum that resulted led to an emphasis on internal and personal values. As a result, the concept of the individual self grew more and more important. The individual, now cut free from his ties and obligations to an organic society, was expected to show moral behavior for its own sake. The concept of character became the basis for moral life. In a post-Enlightenment world where traditional external and absolute values had been undermined, the emphasis was placed on the individual's internal strength to act correctly. However, as the nineteenth century gave way to the twentieth century, character gave way to personality as the dominant personal trait. This represents another example of substance becoming secondary to appearance, which is the root of results being valued over performance.

Warren Susman claims that character started to emerge as an important concept in nineteenth century western culture. He notes that, "By 1800 the concept of character had come to define that particular model type felt to be essential for the maintenance of social order. The term itself came to mean a group of traits believed to have social significance and moral quality . . . "[16]

There appeared at this time a plethora of literary efforts proporting to aid the individual in the pursuit of self-control and self-development, the twin conceptual values of character. Character was the guiding light in all moral and social life. In fact, character linked the moral to the social. Such traits as citizenship, duty, honor, integrity, honesty, and politeness were all facets of character. Ralph Waldo Emerson defined character as, "Moral order through the medium of individual nature."[17]

The function of character is clearly important in a cultural tradition where the previous basis for moral behavior had been destroyed. The concept of character puts the onus on the newly developed, newly pre-eminent self, to uphold standards in society on a moral basis emanating from the individual's strength of character. It is also clear that the values of a culture of character dovetailed neatly with the standards of a Doing culture, forming a most perfect union with the Protestant work ethic. Values such as thrift, hard work, and reliability fit well into a production-oriented society.[18]

Just as Sadler notes that normative behavior changes from production to consumption as Doing shades into Having as a cultural type, Susman identifies parallel changes in the very nature of how the self was viewed. During the eighteenth century, references started to appear in written works to personality as a separate entity from character. By the start of the twentieth century, personality development was the subject of as much literature as character had been in the preceding centuries.[19]

The difference between the terms, character, and personality, are dramatically illustrated by a comparison of the adjectives used to describe them. For example, personalities may be described as magnetic, dominant, fascinating, attractive, creative, and forceful. Character is more likely to be called honest, trustworthy, hardworking, and just. Character is either good or bad, while personality is famous or infamous.[20]

In the culture of personality the problem was no longer how to maintain a moral social order, which was the role of character, but one of how to distinguish oneself in a mass society. The culture of character at least demanded some connection of achievement with fame. The culture of personality makes no such demand, just that of making oneself pleasing to others. Susman suggests that the task contained something of an internal paradox, the need was to distinguish oneself from, yet remain attractive to and please the mob.[21] This is a process represented quite graphically in the emergence of the cinema in the first quarter of the twentieth century; especially in the new techniques of using huge numbers of anonymous extras in massive crowd scenes, which contrasted with the equally new techniques of using very tight "close ups" of the faces of the lead players. This presented on the one hand a featureless mob, and on the other, the huge image of the disembodied face of the star.[22]

The Culture of Narcissism

The tension between the need to differentiate oneself from the mob and the need for its approval is one of the characteristics that Christopher Lasch attributes to the narcissistic personality that he sees as dominating contemporary culture.[23] Lasch describes our contemporary western culture as one of competitive individualism, ". . . which in its decadence has carried the logic of individualism to the extreme of a war of all against all, the pursuit of happiness to the dead end of a narcissistic pre-occupation with self."[24]

The twentieth century development of the culture of narcissism goes hand in hand with the emergence of the concept of celebrity, which replaced the last vestige of character, and replaced personality as the core of contemporary culture in the 1970s. The culture of narcissism represents an intensification of self-aggrandizement and the lack of demand for substance, which is replaced by the appearance of success.

In the culture of narcissism, individuals are not torn by guilt as much as perplexed by anxiety. They seek not to inflict their own certainties on others but to find some basis for certitude. The pervading atmosphere in this culture is therapeutic rather than religious. People do not seek salvation or enlightenment, but the temporal and temporary feelings of safety and normalcy.[25]

Lasch attacks the theraputic for seeking to free the individual, his needs and interests, from all subservience to those of others, some cause, or tradition outside of themselves.[26] In the therapeutic exercise, Lasch claims that meaning and love are viewed merely as the fulfillment of the patient's emotional needs. From these psychiatric and psychological practices grew the new consciousness movements of the

1960s and 1970s searching for self-awareness and self-fulfillment. The failure of personal relationships to provide satisfaction drives the individual deeper into themselves. The reasoning of the self-awareness movements leads individuals to "hold back" in relationships, and not make much commitment to love and friendship as these relationships have proved to be so unsatisfying. But it is just such a lack of sincerity and depth that made the relationships unsatisfying in the first place.[27]

Individuals in the narcissistic culture, as in the Having culture, seek to fill the void in their existence by mandatory consumption. Advertising assures us that our problems can be alleviated by the possession of certain products. Lasch suggests that consumption becomes an alternative to rebellion. Instead of social change there is fashion change, or we acquire some product to brighten our oppressed existence.[28]

One of the concomitant developments of the culture of narcissism is a loss of faith in the future and a devaluing of the past. Lasch attributed the former to the latter. The past is trivialized by associating it with ". . . outmoded styles of consumption, discarded fashions and attitudes."[29] Instead of using the past as a source of experience and knowledge, it is commodified and marketed as nostalgia. Any warm feelings towards the past or identification with it are dismissed as nostalgia as well. As a result of the rejection of the past, there arises an inability to shape and identify needs from personal experience of satisfactions in the past. To the contrary, experts identify the needs, and either supply the answers to these needs themselves, or serve the actual suppliers.[30] This circular process is, of course, the model for contemporary consumer society: create a need and then fulfill it, for a price.

Experts of all kinds, in all fields of knowledge, free individuals from burdens that interfere with their productivity, while at the same time making them consumers of the expert's services. Obstetricians take charge at birth, pediatricians supervise child care, teachers educate, bosses supervise work, supermarkets provide standardized food, television provides standardized beliefs, and so on. We surrender at every turn, in ever increasing situations with ever increasing ease, to a specialized, trained, expert who deals with our problems for us.

The culture of narcissism not only creates needs to be fulfilled but also celebrities to be admired and consumed. The mass media packages the image of the celebrity and creates an aura of glamour and excitement around them. The masses are encouraged to consume these products as fans, moviegoers and spectators. Image is the most important aspect of the culture of narcissism. Achievement is second-ary to the appearance of achievement. "Power lies in the eye of the beholder and as such has no objective reference at all."[31]

The development of the culture of celebrity contrasts with the earlier culture of character in the same way that the culture of personality contracts with that of character. But celebrity seems to be an even more facile value than personality. For while personality demands no worth, just the ability to engraciate oneself with others, celebrity merely requires that one is well-known.

In the eighteenth century version of the work ethic, virtue paid off in a clear conscience at the end of life. Achievement was seen as adding to the accumulated worth of the society. Even in the nineteenth century achievement was measured against abstract standards, not against the achievement of others. However, by the start of the twentieth century, achievement was not enough. One also had to out perform one's peers. "Young men were told that they had to sell themselves in order to succeed."[32] In the culture of narcissism, achieve-ment has become an end in itself, not a means to an end beyond personal material gain. The appearance of success is the goal. Thus, in a society where appearance counts for more than substance, celebrity is more prized than fame. Fame depends on the acclaim of great performances. Celebrity is the reward for those who have attracted attention to themselves, and is perpetuated through the media network of gossip columns, talk shows, magazines, and tabloids devoted to celebrating the worthless. Lasch suggests that as a result of the media's prominent role in the construction of the reality of the culture of narcissism, the real world, outside of media production, seems unreal! "We live in a swirl of images and echoes that arrest experience and play it back in slow motion."[33] We come to distrust our own perception and wait for the media, particularly the camera, to provide validation. Reality is what the camera shows us, and the family photo album confirms our existence.[34]

The Monsters of Emotivism

It is against the background of celebrity worship and rootless values that Alasdair MacIntyre claims that an emotivist morality has grown up and allowed certain "characters" to rise to prominence in contemporary society.

Emotivism is the belief that all moral and ethical judgments are statements of preference, and no more than that. To say, "this is good," is to really say, "I think this is good, so should you." Subjective opinion is presented as fact. But as such, no one assertion is any more valid than another. The Enlightenment had undermined the universal and absolute components of truth, leaving only relative and contingent truth. It has already been shown that the Enlightenment produced great interest in objective truth and achieved what today passes as objectivity in the form of scientific method. But we have also already seen that science is value-blind and cannot give moral guidance. Objective standards could not escape the language of efficiency and effectiveness in achieving ends. Rationality in this narrow sense had become the substitute for morality.

MacIntyre points out that in the pre-Enlightenment organic world, human life had a purpose, a telos. The telos of man was to fulfill his role in society, that role ascribed to him at birth or through position. This was the essence, or true nature of man; to play one's part effectively and faithfully. The loss of such a telos is one of the prices we have paid for the Enlightenment's freedom in the contemporary western world. MacIntyre further claims that the purpose of moral life has been lost in the process. Ethics was the means by which "man as he is", could become "man as he could be if he realized his telos." With the loss of the telos, modernity and contemporary western society is left with "man as he is," and a set of now incomprehensible terms referring to ethics. The language of pre-Enlightenment morality, values, and ethics is still with us today, but it has no reference point in post-Enlightenment life. Man was freed from the ancient authority of absolutes, state and church, but simultaneously he lost the concept of a telos as a member of that type of society.[35]

MacIntyre uses the model of the moral agent as being detached from any social particularity, and passing judgment from a purely abstract and subjective point of view. Under this conception anyone and everyone can be a moral agent, since it is in the self, and not in social roles or practices, that moral agency lies.

"The democratized self which has no necessary social content and no necessary social identity, can then be anything, can assume any role, or take any point of view, because it is and for itself nothing."[36] This anchorless, valueless, and purposeless being is the basis from which emotivism can run wild.

MacIntyre feels that contemporary society is emotivist *de facto* if not *de jure*. In a society with no human or humanizing purpose built on the destruction of absolute natural authority, relativistic authority grew in its place. The contemporary western world is geared to conspicuous consumption and the worship of celebrity, and emotivism represents the obvious moral doctrine to provide the means to that end. Being able to achieve your personal end becomes a virtue; being able to achieve what you want, having the power to achieve what you want, becomes the justification for achieving what you want. Power is its own justification. There is no social framework to channel, control, and judge behavior. There is no appeal to a morality that could deny the legitimacy of your methods or goals because there are no standards that we do not create. The law is the brake on power, but the laws are created out of the emotivist society. Laws prohibit certain acts, and as a result all that is not actually illegal is permissible and cannot be condemned except by another's taste. The fact that laws come out of society means that the powerful within society have a huge input into the formulation of the law. As Phil Elliot says of a massive animal lineman in *North Dallas Forty*, "Joe Bob is here to remind us that the biggest and the meanest get to make all the rules." When his female companion says that she does not agree with that, Phil replies, "Agreement don't enter into it."[37]

In *After Virture*, MacIntyre identifies three "characters" that define the culture of the contemporary society. He uses the term "character" because it suggests dramatic and moral facets that are missing in "social role." He states that in the "character," ". . . role and personality are fused. Social type and psychological type are required to coincide. The character morally legitimates a mode of social existence."[38]

His concept of character leaves no room for conflict between the individual and the role, as is possible between the ordinary individual and his social role. A "character" could never suffer contradiction, like the policeman who steals, or the adulterous priest. This is because ". . . the requirements of the character are imposed from outside, from the way in which others regard and use the character to understand and evaluate themselves."[39] Thus, the "character" supplies a cultural and moral ideal to a significant segment of the society.

The "characters" that MacIntyre identifies as defining the contemporary emotivist society represent a culmination of the flow of history and philosophy that we have been following. He identifies them as "the rich aesthete," "the bureaucratic manager," and "the therapist." The rich aesthete lives a lifestyle of incredible material luxury, the model of consumption. He exists in contemporary society's concept of bliss. As the king of the Having culture, it does not matter how he rose to his status, only that he lives the way he does.

The bureaucratic manager is responsible for efficient organization and administration of production. He is the king in a production oriented society, but the nature of his techniques dehumanize people. MacIntyre claims management is for materials and those methods applied to people become manipulation.[40]

The therapist's role is to return people to health, to fix the broken units of production and consumption and quickly restore them to operation. The therapist uses an approach that objectifies the patient, the very expression "clinical efficiency" portrays an impersonal relationship when there are really few more personal relationships. He represents another form of manipulation, a rationalization of the humane into the mechanical.

In MacIntyre's conception of the contemporary emotivist society, the individual moral agent, with no basis for his agency, is victim of the power and desires of others. He is the means to their ends. Specifically, the individual suffers the manipulations of the bureaucratic manager, while being sustained by the therapist, to chase the dream of the lifestyle of the rich aesthete. In this society, good and bad, right and wrong, are at best expressions of taste, and at worst, comments on the efficacy of means to ends. The weak are the tools of the powerful because they have no reference points save for the "characters." We must work out our own salvation with diligence while the "characters," the purveyors of culture, race after their own interests running rough shod over all others.

When President Reagan addressed an audience of African-Americans in Atlanta on Martin Luther King Jr.'s birthday, it did not matter that Reagan had opposed every civil rights reform that the Reverend had advocated. Reagan's character, what he believed and stood for, did not matter. Reagan was the Presidential personality, he had power, and he had a shining image. When image is more important than substance, questions of right and wrong are no longer central issues. Power is its own justification. Appearance and style are more important than worth and intent.

This is the fine-tuned, high performance emotivist machine. Who better to persuade, someone who is good or someone who looks good? There is then no demand on the perceiver to make an intellectual response, no need to understand and weigh the issues, only to judge appearance and recognize power. In our contemporary culture it is more important to look good than to be good. In contemporary sport it often seems as if it is more important to look good on the scoreboard than to be a good athlete, or a good person.

Summary

This chapter has examined the roots of contemporary values, stemming as they do from the events of the Enlightenment. The evolution of pre-Enlightenment culture into contemporary culture has also been followed from ancient Athens to present day western society.

After the Enlightenment, the individual became central to society. Freed by rational thought and the power of reason, ordinary men built a new world with the scientific method. Despite the success of scientific method at explaining the physical world, it became apparent that science could not fully guide man's existence. The feeling that there was more to being human than science could show gave rise to romantic and transcendental movements. Meanwhile, the true believers of science flowered as reductionists, logical positivists, and formalists.

The moral vacuum left by the failure of the Enlightenment to produce a rational basis for values led to the application of scientific method to human relationships. This became the basis for our de facto emotivism. In the absence of a substantiated moral framework, trying to be good for its own sake has given way to trying to look good for one's own sake.

What started in the Enlightenment as a desire to escape arbitrary control and judgment has developed into a quest for objectification. One of the consequences is that much of the sport world today looks for objective criteria because we no longer recognize what is good. The flow of thought and societal development since the Enlightenment has been a slow and gradual story of the promotion of the individual and the objectification of values. But because values cannot be objective, our contemporary world is a maelstrom of value judgments masquerading as facts. In such an environment the test of athletic excellence lies in the numbers on the scoreboard, with no need for the observer or participant to make a judgment.

The theme of this chapter has been to illustrate the origin of the values of contemporary western culture. The consequences of the evolution of contemporary culture for the development of contemporary sport are examined in the next chapter. The issue of the sports people who cannot differentiate high quality performance from winning, those heirs of the Enlightenment's rationalism, is examined in chapter 3. But both issues are directly based on the evolution of the post-Enlightenment culture described here.

CHAPTER 2

The Development of Contemporary Sport

This chapter outlines the development of contemporary sport and the consequences of this process from an historical point of view. It is my contention that the emergence of contemporary sport results from the forces released in post-Enlightenment western society, characteristically demonstrated in increasing instrumental reason and rationalization. The result is an objectified view of sport performance, culminating in the use of sport as a means to reach external goals, and a devaluing or denial of its internal value. Thus, sport has come to be valued as a means and not as an end in itself. It is a metamorphosis that Allan Guttmann encapsulates in the title of his work, *From Ritual to Record*.[1]

To understand contemporary sport it is necessary to identify and analyze the characteristics of modern sport and examine the commodification of sport under capitalism, rather than modernity. Thus, it can be shown that there is no necessary causal link between the process of modernization and commodified contemporary sport. I will then examine the Marxist and Neo-Marxist critiques of commodified sport and the views of the communist countries, as it initially appears that they might offer an environment in which results are not valued over performance. Finally, the observations of Lasch regarding the impact of modern society on sport are contrasted with those of Johan Huizinga.

Two important points must be made in discussing the evolution of pre-modern sport into modern sport and the emergence of contemporary sport. First, the term contemporary sport is a reference to an actually existing condition, while pre-modern and modern are ideal sport types that are useful in discussing the development of sport. Second, the movement from pre-modern to modern ideal sport types and the development of contemporary sport have both been played out against the backdrop of the maelstrom of values detailed in chapter 1. The analysis of modern sport and the critiques of commodified sport are important because they deal directly with the consequences of post-Enlightenment thought.

The process of the development of pre-modern sport, through various levels of modernization, to commodified contemporary sport illustrates the evolution of sport as a means to external ends. Together with this development there has been a devaluing, or even denial, of the value of sport in itself. The external and objective assessment of the value of sport is closely linked to the objectification of the values in society.

The Modernization of Sport

Although sport and society did not modernize at the same time or rate, the ideal type characteristics of pre-modern and modern sport are closely related to those of pre-modern and modern society. Pre-modern society can be characterized as organic and ascriptive. A society in which one was born into a position, part of a fixed hierarchy in society, which determined relationships between individuals. Pre-modern society was ritualistic and cyclical in nature. The past, present, and future were viewed as part of the same thing; there was no idea of progress. The ritualistic nature of society was reflected in the creation of legends and myths that were taken as fact and used to explain the world.

Modern society is achievement oriented. One works to climb as high as possible, from which position relationships to others are worked out functionally. This contrasts sharply with the ascriptive hierarchy of pre-modern times. In modern society, technology has replaced muscle as the central source of power in the work world. The past, present, and future are differentiated and time is conceived of as being linear. Rationality has replaced ritual as the central theme of society. Modern man defers pleasure into the future as a justification for hardship in the present, while contemporary man finds it rational to consume now and not delay gratification. Rational thought is based on the belief that there is a logical relationship between means and ends, causes and effects, that can be deduced from scientific method. It is wrongly deduced from this principle that we are rational beings when the opposite is actually true.[2]

Modernization is the process of moving from a society exhibiting all of the pre-modern ideal characteristics to one exhibiting all of the modern, ideal characteristics. Modernization is, therefore, a movement along a continuum, and at some point enough modern characteristics are shown for the society to be termed modern. Which is not to say that the society will not further modernize. The same process is true of the modernization of sport.[3]

The characteristics of pre-modern and modern ideal sport types have been identified in the work of both Allan Guttmann and Melvin L. Adelman.[4] The modernization of sport as examined through the ideal types is of great importance to this study as the characteristics are indicative of the changes in post-Enlightenment society, typified by an increasing rationalization and objectification of values in sport. Of the nine different ideal type characteristics that Adelman and Guttman identify, the most important to this study are secularization, equality of opportunity, rationalization, bureacratization, quantification, record-keeping, and the distribution of public information.

Guttman points to the secularization of sport, its loss of religious significance. Adelman does not mention this point because he is addressing the modernization of American sport specifically, and sport in both the colonies and the Republic never had religious significance. Guttman refers to the ritual and religious significance of ceremonial games in some pre-modern societies and suggests that this feature has been lost in modern sport. Some scholars have interpreted sport as a modern natural religion, or as serving religious functions.[5] Guttman does not deny this function but points out, "We do not run in order that the earth be more fertile. We till the earth, or work in our factories and offices, so that we can have time to play."[6] As Donald Mrozek observes, "In practice, though rarely in theory, sport became the religious ritual of the machine age—sacrifice without purpose, performance without magic, obsolescence without compensation, and value without meaning."[7]

Guttman's second point is the theoretical democratization of modern sport. This is manifested in the theoretical base that everyone has an equal opportunity to participate and to compete under equal conditions. Guttman concedes that in practice there are many violations of this ideal, but it is still our expressed ideal. Whereas, in pre-modern society, sport had a ceremonial, ritual, and religious function in which participation had a significance in itself in that it was symbolic of something. In modern sport, the modern societal value of achievement is of central importance, and therefore sport needs to be open to all, and not just to a privileged few. The implementation of actual democracy was one of the major products of the Enlightenment, giving birth through revolution to the French and American Republics. The freedom of the individual to compete has become a basic tenant of modern sport and modern culture.

Adelman does not discuss this factor as American society was founded on equality of opportunity, and therefore, sport in America modernized within an already theoretically equal society. For example, in English pre-modern society, hunting was a major sport, but there were many restrictions on the right of the individual to hunt. Whether and what one could hunt depended upon one's status in society.[8] But in America there was no such class-based limitation on activity. However, we can contrast this interpretation with the view that if equality of opportunity is a characteristic of modernized sport, then America only recently became modern in this sense. Until the 1960s racism was an overt and pervasive force in American society and American sport. In fact there are powerful claims that American society and sport are still racist, but now at least the racism is de facto rather than de jure.[9] That is to say, it may be the way it is, but at least it is not the way we legislate it to be. We could interpret American sport as having failed to fully modernize in this area as it still operates a restrictive participation policy.

The development of universal rules is another characteristic of modern sport identified by Adelman and described as rationalization by Guttman. Pre-modern sports rules were characteristically unwritten and local, having no wide base of implementation. In modern sport, rules are not only written and applied worldwide, but they are also pragmatically worked out and adjusted by organizing bodies. Rationalization is the key characteristic that separates pre-modern and modern ideal cultural types, the former being ritualist and the latter, rationalistic.

Both Guttman and Adelman identify the emergence of bureaucratic organization and the collection of statistics as characteristics of modern sport. In pre-modern American society, sport was of an ad hoc nature, promoted on a local level by villages, tavern owners, and bettors. Today the bureaucracies of sport organizations encircle the globe. There are international organizations made up of national organizations, broken into regional organizations, for almost every sport. These organizations serve a number of functions from rule development to staging world championships.

A further development of modern sport, linked in some way to bureaucratic organization, is the collection of sport statistics. These two developments are very important because they form the basis from which results are valued over performance. The rationalization of life in post-Enlightenment society, where traditional values have been eroded, leaves the objective statistical view of sport as a simple assessment of value. Modern society, particularly modern American society, is marked by a tendency to reduce events to statistics. Whether in the form of the grade point average, earned run average, yards per carry, or the Dow Jones Index, numbers are the ultimate rationalization—the implications and consequences of which are a central theme in this whole study. As Guttman states: "When we can no longer distinguish the sacred from the profane or even the good from the bad, we content ourselves with the minute discrimination between the batting average of the .308 hitter and the .307 hitter."[10]

In his analysis of the modernization of sport, Adelman identifies two further characteristics. One is the availability and dissemination of public information; the other is the changing nature of competition. The development of the sports page in the newspaper, specialist publications, the telegraph, and later radio and television coverage, all served to educate and inform the public. Pre-modern sport news was characterized by oral, local information. This factor is closely linked to the change in the nature of competition. This change is reflected in the national, and indeed international, nature of sport. It is now possible to build a reputation in sport competition that spreads worldwide. The relevance of the growth of sport media is linked to the culture of personality and celebrity discussed in chapter 1. In contemporary sport it is largely through the vehicle of the media that an athlete's image is formed and projected. In fact, the power of the media to make "stars" is a central contribution to the problem of values in sport, the continual aggrandizement of winners, and the subsequent illegitimate transfer of the meaning of winning in sport to an assertion of general human superiority.

We could encapsulate these factors of modernization in an imaginary, but not unlikely, example. A working-class man, a specialist athlete, might have his performance quantified and declared a world record by the governing body of his sport. Subsequently, news of his feat spreads around the world to those who did not see it live on television, and he is instantly made internationally famous; an instant celebrity. This would have been inconceivable in pre-modern society and equally so in pre-modern sport.

It must be pointed out that modernization is a sweeping term. When one sport has progressed sufficiently along the continuum between pre-modern and modern society to be termed modern, is all sport then modern? No, different sports modernize at different rates. Harness racing, for instance, had progressed far enough to be termed modern by the mid-nineteenth century.[11] This is not to say that harness racing did not continue to modernize into the twentieth century. Football and basketball, on the other hand, did not modernize until well into the twentieth century.

The Distinction Between Modernization and Commodification

Modern sport is not entirely a twentieth century phenomenon. A distinction must be made between the hyper-commercialization and commodification of sport that exploded in the mid-twentieth century and the modernization of sport that had been in progress since the mid-nineteenth century. The changes in sport that occurred around 1940 reflected an expansion of the move from a production orientation to a consumption orientation in American society. Sport was turned into another commodity to be consumed, it was commodified. While it is true to a certain extent of all professional sport throughout history, this period exhibits an extreme intensification of commodification. Professional and college sports events became increasingly subject to marketing and management rationales. The pleasure of the player became secondary to that of the spectator. The trappings of the various sports, replica uniforms, balls, bats, souvenirs, etc., began to be mass-produced and marketed to fans and course players.

During this period, television became the dominant force in the development of sport. In the case of professional football, people in the stands were no longer the most important source of revenue as the game was already sold to television companies and paid for by advertisers.[12] The sports fan of today who wishes to see the event need not even be a spectator; he can be a viewer. Television can make a leisurely, insulated, voyeur of him, free from even the commitment of travel time and monetary outlay, and at the same time deny him the spectator's marginal role as a participant. Commodification is not a definitive requirement for a sport to be termed modern. It is something that happened to modern sport. That is to say, it is not a necessary stage of modernization, although it could be interpreted as a product of the process. We can have modernization without commodification, but it is hard to imagine commodification without modernization.[13]

When we talk casually of modern sport we often have in mind the image of televised, commercialized, and commodifed sport. But sport was modern before these events and various sports are continuing to modernize. When we talk casually of the evils of modern sport we are really talking of commodifed sport. Today in the West we are all moderns, and to fail to see that can lead to much misdirected effort and resentment. It is a mistake to think that we should want to return to pre-modern times. What we must do is save modernity not dream of escaping it. The nature of pre-modern sport is alien to us today. What some people long for are the days of player centered sport. Modernization is not the villain in today's sport. If there is a villain it is commodification.

The Marxist View of Commodified Sport

The single greatest critic of the process of commodification of experience by the capitalist rationale is Karl Marx. It is to the Marxist and Neo-Marxist view of sport to which we must now turn.

There is a Marxist view of sport in much the same way that there is a Platonist view of sport, in as much as neither Marx nor Plato addressed themselves specifically or directly to sport. Rather, what is offered as the Marxist and Platonist view of sport is an extrapolation from the works of these masters by those who followed them. Physical educators, for example, have seized on rather shallow readings of Plato, particularly of the *Republic*, to try and find historical/philosophical justification for their own discipline. Similarly, different readings of Marx have, on one extreme, led to the rejection of modern sport, and on the other extreme, the glorification and promotion of sport, both citing Marx as their authority.[14]

Karl Marx addressed himself to the major problems of modern mid-nineteenth century life. He was greatly influenced by Hegel and Feuerbach, aspects of whose works he fused in his own Dialectialcal Materialism.[15] This concept combines the Hegelian Dialectic and the Historical Materialism of Feuerbach. The former being the concept that every thesis contains its own antithesis, and that the two conflict and then merge to create a new and greater reality.[16] The latter concept is based on economic determinism, and holds that a society's mode of economic production determines the nature of its culture and social structure. At the heart of this position is Marx's belief that there is an intimate relationship between matter and mind, and that the former largely determines the latter.[17]

"It is not the consciousness of man that determines their being, but, on the contrary, their social being that determines their consciousness."[18]

Marx was not content to be a philosopher since he believed that philosophers only interpret the world. He wanted to change it. Above all else, Marx wanted to end capitalist exploitation of the workers and put the ownership of the means of production into the hands of the workers. The effect of the capitalistic economic system was to alienate the worker from his work and develop a false consciousness. Marx describes this process as, "The science of denial," and goes on, "The more you save the greater will become that treasure . . . your capitol. The less you are, the less you give expression to your life, the more you have, the greater your alienation."[19]

Marx's basic position has implications for sport. Whereas, to the liberal capitalist society, concerned as it is with individuality, sport is ". . . a feature of life unconnected with classes and social values, with economics and society's mode of production; little attention will be paid to it as a social phenomenon."[20] To the Marxist, sport is not a thing in itself, separate from politics; it is founded on class relationships and modes of production.

Marx's materialism opposes a mind/body dualism in that it reduces everything to the material as an explanation of reality. The body is not seen as inherently inferior to the mind. Although early Marxists ignored the body in favor of intellectual theories, it was not until the Neo-Marxists applied this intellectual rigor to the body that a real Marxist view of sport emerged. Marx stressed that all practical activities have an important effect on human development, notably work, through which people could change themselves and nature.[21]

Marx's materialism raises two crucial issues for this study. First, Marx takes the position that social existence shapes consciousness, and second, that practical activities have an important influence on people and the world. It would seem that these are contradictory points. If our social activities and organization determine our consciousness, how then can we change ourselves and our world through our activities? Which effects which? Does society determine consciousness? How then can we change ourselves and our world through our activities, if they have already determined our consciousness? This apparent contradiction comes from Marx's use of the word "determines" in the phrase, "social being determines their consciousness." Perhaps the situation would be clearer if the qualifying clause "if we let it" is added. Marx denies the element of individual choice. The capitalistic exploitation of the worker does not necessarily alienate him from his craft and his true nature, but it does make it harder for him to maintain an unalienated relationship to his craft, and provides no incentive to nurture such a relationship.[22]

The idea that our activities and our attitude to those activities can affect our existence is central to this study. If we allow our social being to determine our consciousness, we will never be able to escape the claim that results are more important than performance. The way to escape this situation lies in the belief that we create our own social being, a view that will be addressed in later chapters through the stance of playfulness and the views of Nietzsche and Rorty. The importance of our relationship to our activities is expressed in Alasdair MacIntyre's concepts of the internal good of a practice and its relationship to institutions. This, too, becomes a central theme later in this narrative.

Marx held the view that, in a truly communist society, work would be elevated to the level of play by the removal of compulsion and alienation. However, different scholars have interpreted Marx's position on play/labor as either antithetical or dialectical. If play and labor are taken as dialectical, then play can be seen as the creative element of work. A dialectical view expounds the suggestion that the unalienated worker will find his work to be play-like, when the capitalistic system no longer suppresses the play elements intrinsic to it.[23]

Lasch offers an interpretation of the removal of the play element from work in his article, "The Degradation of Work, and the Apotheosis of Art." He suggests that the creative, playful, artistic elements that exist in unalienated work have been promoted into a specialization called art. Capitalistic society has specialists to be creative and expressive called artists. The achievements of the worker are degraded and trivialized. As a remedy for this situation Lasch calls for the return of art to the work place as Marx calls for unalienated praxis.[24]

Marxist Sport: Rhetoric and Reality

It would seem reasonable to expect that allegedly Marxist states would be more likely to support a concept of sport that would preserve the intrinsic values of sport and avoid using it as a means to external ends. Such a view would be in tune with valuing performance as least as highly as results. However, an examination of the major communist countries shows that this is not the case.

It must be remembered that Marx wrote as a theorist of labor, rather than a theorist of leisure. He did not live to see the age of mass sport and leisure and, as a result, he never had to face their bourgeois corruption. Marx never had to deal with sport as an opiate, rather than a recovery from labor.

After Marx's death there emerged, in Marxist thought, an ambivalence to the body. Marx himself did not address sport, play, or sex directly and, in fact, the irrational aspects of existence are still problematic for Marxists today. Hoberman suggests that this is mainly due to the overwhelming intellectuality of the Marxist tradition. A tradition which differentiates ideologically from fascist thought, fascism tries to conquer the rational, to overcome and escape it. The Marxist seeks an intellectual superiority rather than a physical one through the rational training of the faculties.[25]

It was left to those who followed Marx to deal with sport directly, and it is at this point that the waters become muddy. The work of Marx was carried on by Lenin in Russia, and later into the whole European Communist Block. Mao produced his own brand of Marxism in China, and Neo-Marxists of Western Europe produced their own sport theories in the 1960s.

The Soviets and their satellites have produced a rhetoric that denounces capitalistic sport as exploitative and dehumanizing. The fact that the athlete may actually seek this exploitation is a symptom of their false consciousness, produced by their alienated state. Capitalistic sport is also criticized for its lack of concern for the injury it causes to participants. For example, professional boxing is heartily condemned for its danger, commodification which destroys its value as a sport, and the unwholesome nature of its entertainment, titillation, and gratification. The Soviets see a real distinction between the sport of amateur boxing, and the capitalist exploitation of professional boxing.[26]

The Soviets are also violently opposed to exhibitionism and narcissism in sport and society. This idea exists in a state of tension with that of the star performer as an edifying figure, as an educator. The danger is that the star will become seduced by his own achievements and fall into an antisocial egocentric state. Physical culture combined with competitive sport is seen as a way to politically socialize the population. The Soviets promote the idea of "universal sport", which makes sport participation available to both sexes, all ages, and all occupations. They are seeking what Marx called the "new socialist man."[27]

The other main communist state offering a living interpretation of Marxist thought is communist China, where Marxist sport culture can be divided into two distinct phases: Maoist, 1950-1976, and post-Maoist, after 1976. Maoist sport promoted a unique etiquette based on the eradication of hostile or aggressive feelings towards an opponent. It was an etiquette that applied equally to winning and losing, and one which sometimes infuriated foreign opponents who did not understand it. However, an obsessive politeness is a mark of Confucian China, rather than a Marxist idea per se. Maoist sport also emphasized hygienic sport and de-emphasized competition in favor of mass participation. Maoist sport placed no emphasis on the development of super athletes.[28] Instead there was a continued bias towards the collective ideology, which certainly did not allow the sport champion to emerge as an exemplary or edifying figure.[29] Sheer performance was not allowed to triumph over collective ideals.

After Mao's death his successor, Hua Kuo-feng, called for Chinese athletes to produce world class performances. There was a subsequent emphasis on developing top flight performers through sport schools and the use of foreign expert instructors. The etiquette ideal has been somewhat lost today for Chinese athletes as more and more emphasis has been placed on winning.[30]

The Neo-Marxist of West Germany and France produced the first specific, and in depth, Marxist view of sport in the mid-1960s. The student revolts in both of these countries combined with the emergence of the Frankfurt School theorists gave rise to a critical theory of sport. Both these Neo-Marxist groups rejected the alienating effect of the ". . . absolutized performance principle which is sport's purest expression."[31] Capitalistic sport, with its achievement and competitive emphasis, is seen as conflicting with the play spirit that is idealized in the Neo-Marxist critique as a utopian criterion. The West German Neo-Marxist scholars express the ludic in sport as a utopian ideal, while the French developed the ludic in culture as a whole.[32]

Modern leisure is seen as a compensation for and as a distraction from everyday life. This is taken to be necessary because the world of everyday life is unauthentic and alienating. But bourgeois leisure is equally alienating and inauthentic, and appeals only to false consciousness according to the Neo-Marxists. Hoberman comments that;

> In other words, social existence is a seamless whole which cannot be sub-divided into spheres of different existential value in the manner of cultural conservatives like Huizinga. Social life is free 'in toto', or is unfree in the same manner. There is no privileged or transcendental area.[33]

The Neo-Marxists exalt the body as a sphere of pleasure and freedom. Herbert Marcuse speaks of, ". . . the release of the repressed body, instrument of labor and of fun, in a society which is organized against its liberation."[34] The capitalistic society is organized into types of specialization, division of labor, limiting man's possibilities and reducing his opportunity for creativity and self expression.[35] "Man becomes an interchangeable part on the playing field as in the office and the factory . . . man becomes a kind of machine and his movements, controlled by apparatus, become mechanical."[36]

To Neo-Marxists, the Olympic games, for example, do not represent the flowering of sportive freedom but the ultimate in sportive repression and manipulation. The athletes become pawns in nationalistic displays of rationalized competition. Manufactured and dehumanized, the athletes are seen as crippled potentialities.

Finally, the Neo-Marxists view sport as an instrument for socializing the masses into accepting the repressive nature of capitalistic class structure. Sport is inherently unfair and unjust, they argue, with the individual forced to follow rules that are dictated to him and through which the privileges of the ruling class are preserved.

The Neo-Marxists are looking for a new culture of the body, in an authentic totality, that re-establishes the body in all its dimensions. This is a position that not only runs counter to the Marxist tradition but also sounds virtually fascistic. So indeed it would be were it not for the intellectual power of the Neo-Marxist approach. They are not seeking an escape from rationality in bodily expression, but in fact, intellectualize the body and analyze it as a function of the social reality which created it.

This Neo-Marxist intellectualism is best represented by Theodor Adorno and Roland Barthes. Despite showing striking similarities in their critiques of bourgeois culture, they offer very different conclusions about sport. Barthes, unlike Adorno, is able to separate the sphere of the body as a dehumanized cultic space, and sport as a valuable form of social life.[37] Adorno, on the other hand holds that the nature of sport as a manipulation of the individual makes it a structure of the "realm of unfreedom."[38]

The Soviet and Maoist versions of Marxist sport began as revolutionary cultures, an alternative to bourgeois sport. Their goal was to build a sport culture free from ruthless competition, unprincipled appeals to lower desires, and from the socially destructive cult of the star performer. But today communist states are almost as susceptible to a Neo-Marxist critique of their sport culture as capitalistic ones. As James Riordan observes, "Sport in the Soviet Union is by no means a matter of fun and games, it is not the 'garden' of human activities. Physical culture is on a par with mental culture and has important functions to discharge."[39] In this way Soviet sport is linked to outside goals, it is a means to a goal outside of its own value.

The greatest difference between communist and capitalist sport is, of course, that the communist athlete is not being exploited by the team owner. He is thus not alienated from his work by a capitalistic system that engenders a false consciousness in him. For this Marx would be grateful. On the other hand, the Communists indulge in many of the evils associated with capitalistic sport. This can be explained as a function of several factors. The first is that the Soviets betrayed Marx when Stalin came to power. Many contradictions between rhetoric and practice date from the swapping of a ideologist, Lenin, with a power hungry politician with no sense of human value, Stalin. Under Stalin in the 1930s, the emphasis of Soviet society turned from the fraternal to hierarchical. This gave rise to the cult of the heroic laborer, the Stankovite, an individual who overachieves in the name of socialism and becomes a direct model for the record-breaking athlete.[40]

Given that the Soviets have implemented many of Marx's ideas, they are still not a Marxist society simply because they are not free to act and speak in a way compatible with Marx's ideas of personal fulfillment. Changing the mode of production has not proven sufficient to liberate the workers.

In their sport culture the Soviets may not be contaminated by capitalistic perversion, but they are committed to representational sport in intense competition. Allan Guttmann claims that it is representational sport that creates much of the corruption and violence in sport.[41]

A representational sport is one in which the athlete realizes he represents his town, state, or country, and the spectators feel that the athlete is representing them against another group. The Soviets may have socialized industry, they may have socialized sport, and they may have freed their athletes from the alienation of capitalistic sport but, they compete at an international level and adopt a relentless "winning is everything" attitude. This is the ghost in the Soviet sport machine. They apply a capitalistic rationalization to the production of high quality representational teams. Soviet sport is a manufactured commodity, but it is not sold for profit, just for cost! For whatever reason, propaganda is, of course, one the Soviets are desperate to show superiority and technological ability in the metaphorical battle of sport. To this end they have sinned against Marx, and the Neo-Marxists clearly show them doing so. If the Communist countries were truly Marxist they would not compete with capitalist countries, because in so doing they give support to the overall capitalistic system. Nietzsche warned us over a hundred years ago that, "Men who fight with monsters must be careful that they do not become monsters."[42] Modern Communist states have fought with the monsters of capitalism and have themselves become monsters. The theoretical possibilities of the Marxist critique of commodified sport thus remain unfulfilled. While the communist block countries offer a rhetoric of unalienated sport, their manipulation and exploitation of sport to an outside end produces different but equally horrifying excesses as those of capitalistic commodification. Thus, a situation where it might be expected that performance would be valued over results proves barren.

The Capitalist Commodification of Sport

In the shadow of the Enlightenment, modern sport and modern society combined to produce commodified sport. In the moral vacuum that modernity grew out of, the failure to recognize that sport is worthwhile in itself, has allowed the capitalistic spirit to use sport as yet another means to the end of capital accumulation. The commodification of sport is an expression of the capitalistic spirit. Nowhere is this more evident than in the United States. Here the capitalistic spirit demands commodification of all areas of life. The whole of existence is packaged and sold for profit.[43]

The statement that American sport has expressed the capitalistic spirit is interpreted differently in a naive understanding of capitalism than in a more sophisticated understanding. On a naive level, "capitalistic spirit" in American sport is seen as free democratic competition where the winners are rewarded financially for their achievements and the whole enterprise is financed from the takings at the turnstiles and from television contracts. At this level, "capitalistic spirit" means the "American way."

At a more sophisticated level the "capitalistic spirit" is seen as the controlling influence on the evolution of American sport, ". . . in close conformity with the requirements of capital investment and accumulation."[44] Marx and Weber classically claim that the "capitalistic spirit" is manifested throughout modern industrial civilization in the ascendancy of technological and economic rationality as the regulatory principle of all social life.[45]

Rationality is used here in the Weberian sense, referring to the most technically efficient means to an end. All personal and emotional considerations are eliminated from social organization in this rationalization process. What the "capitalistic spirit" comes down to is that the interests of the owners and financiers in American sport largely have come to determine what form technological and economic progress would take. At this level "capitalistic spirit" means the "American way."

It may appear initially that we are talking only of professional sport, but it will become apparent that professionalism is not identical with capitalism, anymore than amateur sport is immune from capitalistic manipulation. The dichotomy is not between professional and amateur, but between objective and subjective value, between treating sport and athletes as means or as ends. Furthermore, it is apparent that, from an early time, the capitalistic spirit in American sport has been opposed to free and democratic competition. The practice of free market liberalism often runs counter to the most rational and effective demands of capital accumulation and thus counter to capitalism itself.

The capitalistic spirit manifested itself in many ways throughout the development of modern sport and its evolution into contemporary sport. In America, notable examples can be found in baseball, football, and the emergence of intercollegiate and professional sport. In his historical overview of American sport, Benjamin G. Rader notes that American sport moved through three stages; the age of folk games, 1607-1850; the age of the player, 1850-1920; and the age of the spectator, 1920-present day.[46] However, it would seem that an analysis of American sport into eras of pre- and post-capitalistic rational cuts across Rader's categories. Undoubtedly, the age of folk games predates the emergence of the capitalistic rationals as equally obviously the age of the spectator post dates it. The emergence of the capitalistic rationale comes somewhere in Rader's "age of the player." The 1850-1920 period contains elements of folk games and new modern sports. In this period, sport was promoted for health reasons, used for social control, became an instrument of Americanization, and a unifying American experience. But sport also became an instrument of class differentiation. Rader claims that this period was dominated by the players. But the period is so long, and so dynamic, that his statement is a sweeping generalization. Well before the turn of the century baseball was no longer player dominated, yet, it is equally clear that football was still player dominated until well after the turn of the century. While the developmental stages Rader uses are useful and valid, they must be applied to individual sports and not to American sport as a whole.

Taking baseball, as an example, the sport certainly was player centered from 1850-1876. This period saw the emergence of baseball as the dominant team sport in America. Players organized the clubs and the leagues, and as these grew to professional status the players initially retained control. The first all-professional league, the National Association of Professional Baseball Players, was formed in 1871. By 1876 capitalistic rationalization made its first appearance in American sport. The interests of the players fell victim to those of the owners in their desire to maximize profits. In a NAPBBP league meeting that year, William A. Hulbert, president of the Chicago club, spoke for a group of dissatisfied club representatives. He reviewed the weaknesses of the NAPBBP and proposed the formation of a new league, the National League of Professional Baseball Clubs. The constitution of the new National League gave the owners of the clubs complete control of management, and in one short meeting, professional baseball went from an association of players to a league of clubs.[47] This 1876 date is the zenith of the player age in baseball, and it certainly did not take baseball another forty-five years to reach the age of the spectator. "The National League pioneered in developing a business structure that would become the standard for all twentieth century team sports. In economic terms, the league was a loosely-organized cartel, an arrangement among the clubs designed to restrict competition among franchises for players."[48] Thus, the capitalistic rationalization exhibited in baseball was in direct conflict with democratic competition.

The National League instituted rules prohibiting the establishment of more than one franchise in each market area irrespective of its size. Further, no club could be set up in a town of less than 75,000 people. The league also established an entry monopoly whereby two existing franchises could "blackball" a new applicant. It soon became clear to the owners that these restrictive practices were not making an impact on their greatest expense: the wages of the players. The owners further realized that it was the competition they created between themselves for the services of the players that was driving the wages higher. The league did ban negotiating with another club's players during the season, but this was not a very effective measure. In 1879, the owners came up with the crowning glory of capitalistic rationality in sport, the reserve clause.[49]

The reserve clause was designed not only to stop competition between the clubs for players from forcing up wages but also to reduce the advantage that the wealthier clubs enjoyed in free market bidding for players. The reserve clause gave the clubs a continuous option on the services of a player. When a contract was signed, the player committed to the club for the period of the contract, plus the club had the option of reserving the player for the following season. Thus, as each succeeding contract also contained the reserve clause, a player could be tied to a club for his whole career by a one year contract. As soon as a player signed with a club he lost his right to bargain and sell his services to the highest bidder. If a player refused to sign the contract offered by his club, no other club could sign him. Unless he could come to some terms with his own club, his career came to a halt or even ended.[50]

The clubs, on the other hand, could terminate a contract at will, and buy and sell players to and from other clubs without the players' consent. The reserve clause gave the clubs property rights to the players, a classic example of capitalist rationalization, reducing a man to a piece of equipment. Although, in contemporary sport it seems as though everytime the courts give professional players freedom of contract, they trade away this freedom for short-term profit.

By 1920 football was moving into its own age of the spectator. It grew from a student interest in northeastern universities to a commercial spectacle of national proportions.[51] New concrete football stadiums sprung up all over the country, and winning football teams had already become potent symbols for their colleges. A winning team promised revenue and fame for the educational institution that it represented. However, the lust for success and its rewards produced a disregard for how it was achieved. This has proved a threat to academic standards and values ever since.

College football players and college football teams are amateur, but college football is organized to capitalistic ends. The overriding effect of the need for success was a disregard for rules. In fact, it seems to have led to a widespread belief that college football transcends all rules. An horrendous example unfolded at Southern Methodist University in 1988. The Governor of Texas, formerly President of the Board of Regents at SMU, was involved in making cash payments to football players at the school. As the NCAA investigation proceeded, more and more violations came to light. The Governor's reaction was to protest that SMU was being persecuted.[52] Persecution, however, is for the innocent, for the guilty it's called justice. The NCAA had been granted power to punish violators of the rules after World War II, but it has proved virtually impossible to detect most violations, let alone punish them.

Professional football emerged in the 1920s but it was not until after World War II that it really exploded on the American sports scene. Professional football was to be the major beneficiary of the dominant force in post-war sport, television. The money television offered made it imperative for team owners and leagues to make their sport as marketable as possible. Professional football offers a clear case of this phenomenon. As John J. Sewart points out;

> During the 1970s, professional football was criticized as being a 'boring' game, i.e., defensive. Stadia across the country became only partly filled and TV ratings dropped to an all time low. The NFL responded with a series of new marketing devices primarily in the form of rule changes and technical innovations.[53]

The owners and the league naturally maintained that the changes were for the protection of the players and that any increase in the spectacular nature of the game was coincidental. A real interest in the players' safety would have led to quite different rule changes such as, a no blitz rule and mandatory man to man coverage which would eliminate a lot of the hits from "nowhere", typical of zone defense.[54]

Further evidence of the capitalist rational in football can be found in society's complicity. Modern professional club owners not only have a legal monopoly, as protected by the 1922 Supreme Court antitrust ruling, but incredibly soft tax laws enabling them to depreciate the value of their players against profits. The net result is that a healthy profit can be shown as a huge loss on the tax forms. Finally, the vast multimillion dollar stadiums that the professional teams inhabit are often built by municipalities who rent them to the clubs at 'sweetheart' rates.[55] The modern owner may not make as much money from his sport franchise as from his other investments, but no other investment makes someone an instant celebrity and no other investment has so many areas of society accommodating their efforts to make money.

There are two significant consequences of sport in America exhibiting the capitalistic spirit. First, sport has become a commodity to be marketed at maximal profit levels, and the internal structure of sport reflects a rationalization favoring the needs of capital accumulation. The second consequence is best expressed in Michael Oriard's distinction between what sport is and what it means. He discusses this dichotomy in relation to football, but it applies equally well to modern sport in general. What sport "is" can be found described above as the first consequence of the capitalistic spirit in sport. Sport is a modern entertainment commodity based on paying spectators viewing highly skilled performers engaged in contests for prizes. What sport "means" is reflected in the significance and value attached to it by society, including the players and spectators.[56]

Sport as a commodity is the result of the capitalistic rationalization process under which all human activity is reduced to labor and subject to market forces. Subsequently, no activity is qualitatively distinct from any other. All activities come to be organized in terms of efficiency and means to the end of capital accumulation.[57]

"In other words the commodity form (sport) no longer satisfies or fulfills a need. The commodity, as an object and product to be exchanged and consumed is separate from the realm of meaningful human interaction. *The commodity becomes experience itself.*"[58] (My emphasis.)

The devaluing, or even erradication, of the affective domain in commodified sport denies the meaning that many people see in sport. Many scholars have acknowledged the mythological aspects of baseball and football, but the damage done to these myths from the ongoing spectacularization of sport has not been addressed as fully.[59] Oriard makes a strong statement about these effects in his work on football, but again, his comments apply to all corporate interests in modern American sport: the NFL, NCAA, NL, NHL, NBA, MISL, PGA, et al.

> Perhaps the powers that run the NFL simply do not understand the nature of the game. Perhaps they have become so concerned with packaging and marketing it that they have forgotten it is not merely a product to be pressed on consumers, but a sport that for many Americans has value and meaning unrelated to its investment potential. Perhaps the NFL will slowly but surely kill football because it forgot, or never knew, what football truly means.[60]

Contemporay Sport: Trivialized or Apotheosised?

Many scholars have approached the meaning and importance of sport through the medium of play. The most celebrated perhaps is Johan Huizinga in his seminal work, *Homo Ludens*. Huizinga suggests that the history of Western culture appears to consist of the gradual elimination of the play element from everyday life. The rationalization of religion, law, social relationships, and above all, work, has removed elements of chance, daring, and uncertainty from everyday life. These characteristics arc, of course, commonly associated with play. Huizinga contends that modern industry has reduced most work to a dull routine, devoid of creativity and craftsmanship. The featureless drab landscape of the modern work life, rational and mechanical, in its bureaucratic miasma, drives people to seek their escape in the play world. Huizinga attributes the incredible importance attached to play today, particularly in the game form, to the desire to escape the everyday.

Huizinga's position is compatible, if not synonymous, with the criticism of commodified sport. He claims that the commercial exploitation of sport has turned play into work, subordinated the pleasure of the athlete to that of the spectator, and at the same time, reduced the spectator to a passive consumer of media images.[61] He describes this development as ". . . a fatal shift towards over-seriousness."[62] Simultaneous with this he maintains that the play element is being divorced from the ritual content of sport. Sport has become detached from society in that the organic communion of sport and structure of society has been severed. Sport has become mere spectacle in which the masses seek ". . . trivial recreation and crude sensationalism."[63]

Christopher Lasch re-examines Huizinga's position and the common misconceptions in his criticism of contemporary sport. Lasch wishes to make more of the distinction between ritual and spectacle. He points out that the critics of modern sport concentrate on its intrinsic elements, spectatorship, violence, and competition. These are then mistakenly attributed to modern sport alone. Huizinga's accusation that modern sport is over-serious is taken by these critics to be central in the historical and contemporary development of sport. Lasch's point is that this critique overlooks the distinctive contribution of modern society to the degradation of sport.[64]

Lasch takes as an example the criticism that modern sports are spectator oriented instead of player centered. He contends that this view holds that spectators are irrelevant to the success of the game. However, he counters that the spectators bear witness to the performance, and their appreciation forges a bond between the athlete and the crowd. Display and representation constitute a central element of sport. The players not only compete, they also enact a familiar ceremony that reaffirms common values. Ceremony requires witnesses: enthusiastic spectators conversant with the rules of performance and its underlying meaning. Far from destroying the values of sport, the attendance of spectators makes them complete.[65]

It is commodification of the event that compromises the values, expanding the audience through television and diluting the quality of the understanding of the audience. The ceremonial and ritualistic elements of sport are sacrificed to larger audiences and increased profits. "Television has rearranged the athletic calendar and thus deprived sports of their familiar connections with seasons, diminishing their power of allusiveness and recall."[66]

Lasch feels that the corruption of athletic performance is not the result of professionalism or competition, but the breakdown of the conventions surrounding the game. "It is at this point then that ritual, drama, and sport all degenerate into spectacle . . . The degeneration of sport then consists not in its being taken too seriously but in its trivialization."[67]

Contrary to Huizinga's view, Lasch attributes the corruption of sport to a lack of seriousness not an over-seriousness. Huizinga resents modern sport for its loss of ritualistic significance and its over-seriousness. Lasch resents modern sport for failing to retain its modern ritualistic significance and collapsing into spectacle.

The power of play and games resides in their illusion of seriousness, once the illusion is lost then play, games, and sport just become more activities. They become products to be marketed and trivialized because they are not serious. The illusion is undermined by players, promoters, and media alike. Players define themselves as entertainers; promoters encourage the creation of spectacular events such as, half-time shows and fireworks displays, all of which detract from the centrality and seriousness of the game. The spectacle becomes more important than the event, like a day at Disney World where all is superficial and we know it is not real. The media in its spirit of debunking takes every opportunity to expose the ordinary and fallible in sport.

Michael Novak claims that the invasion of sport by the entertainment ethic brings the play world of sport back to the drudgery of the everyday.[68] However, Lasch takes a very different tack, and claims that sport is reduced to a spectacle by the invasion of the entertainment ethic resulting from the attempt to create a separate play world. The use and conception of play as a world of escape from the work world cuts it off from cultural significance. As a separate world of escape, play can no longer ". . . dramatize reality and offer a convincing representation of community values."[69]

The same rationalization of the work world has been applied to the play world. From Lasch's view, Novak fails to see that the degradation of sport comes from the degradation of work. The attempt to escape from the drudgery of work resulted in the creation of commercialized recreation as an alternative.

As Huizinga points out, it is when play is lost from the everyday world in the process of rationalization that men seek to escape into a separate world of play. But the creation of a separate play realm does not result in its becoming over-serious, as Huizinga claims, but in its trivialization.

Summary

It is the subservience of sport to other ends that produces a cultural setting that values the result over the performance. In this chapter I have examined the emergence of modern sport and how it can be distinguished from commodified sport. The Marxist views of sport and the rhetoric of the nominally Marxist states of the Eastern Block have been explored. Sport in the United States was examined as the quintessence of commodification. But it must be remembered that all of these views of sport—Marxist, Soviet, and Capitalist—are modern views. They are all products of Enlightenment thought. While the Neo-Marxist critique does try to explain the damage done in commodified sport, both the Soviet and Capitalist practices exploit sport to some other end and thus represent a further use of instrumental reason.

The rhetoric of winning as the test of excellence grows out of the cultural setting where the content of the activity is secondary to that which it can be used for: money, power, or propaganda. As Lasch points out, the problem is not that sport is taken too seriously, but that it is not taken seriously enough to retain its own value as an end in itself.

CHAPTER 3

The Consequences of Contemporary Values for Sport

This chapter examines the philosophical consequences of the unfolding of Enlightenment thought for the world of sport. Given the reductionist and positivistic flavor of contemporary culture, it is not surprising that the model of achievement and value of sport is "objective". The scoreboard and the record book have become the final determinants of worth and value. Although sport represents staggering feats of physical prowess and explosive brilliance, contemporary society looks at a scoreboard to tell them who is most worthy, who is excellent. James Keating is representative of those who subscribe to this view of values and excellence in sport, and equates winning with excellence, a view that stems directly from the flow of post-Enlightenment thought. Keating is writing out of the tradition of post-Enlightenment thought, and his position is a direct extension of the rationality which is the central characteristic of the Enlightenment. Both rationality and reason have become essentially means to ends. They are the tools to get what you want, rather than to help you discover what you want, indeed, what you should want.

If no alternative can be supported and winning becomes necessarily equated with excellence, then this study fails. If no escape can be found from the concept of winning as excellence, then there can be no basis for opposing the valuing of results over performance and image over actual achievement. The task at present is to show that Keating's view is not necessarily accurate and to establish the basis of an alternative view of excellence in sport.

Winning as Excellence

Keating states that there is perhaps no clearer manifestation of the pursuit of excellence than in the athletic contest. He claims it was

47

there that the western world first became enamored with the quest for excellence. He argues that Homeric heroes understood life as a contest, and to prove themselves the best was the object of their existence. Furthermore, the Homeric hero did not seek excellence as its own reward but as a route to fame and material reward in the form of prizes.[1]

Keating further distinguishes excellence from other terms often regarded as its equivalent such as merit, virtue, and perfection. "Excellence applies to any quality or feature in which the person or thing excels or surpasses all others . . . (but) carries no implication that he or it is without fault, blemish or defect."[2] He concludes that the term excellence denotes favorable comparison with others determined by some test or contest. He claims that "the essence of the athletic endeavor lies in the pursuit of excellence through victory in the contest."[3] Keating's definition deliberately excludes accidental or incidental excellence of all kinds. This point is highlighted by his emphasis on the "pursuit" of excellence.[4]

"Thus when we say that the athlete is engaged in the pursuit of excellence there is no mistaking his goal, he is seeking victory in the contest, his goal is to exceed the achievements of his opponents."[5]

Keating acknowledges the high price to be paid in the pursuit of excellence, the hard work and sacrifices that are demanded. He uses this as a base from which to claim that "doing one's best" is not enough. "Doing one's best," is a concept rooted in *a priori* knowledge of one's limits, or in the expectation of defeat.[6] Keating suggests that reasoned and realistic assessments of one's potential are limiting in that they are premised by an acknowledgment of one's limitations. He seems to advocate a vulgar Nietzschean "will to power" in athletic performance; he supports his case by quoting the anonymous coach's cliche, "The team that won't be beat can't be beat."

This last quote clearly touches a nerve, speaking directly to that inner strength that sport people have all felt, or worse, come up against. But there is something wrong with Keating's usage. The act of reaching down inside oneself for that determination not to lose is part of "doing one's best" expressing the same sentiment but in stronger terms, so the point becomes moot.

However, Keating further claims that "The chief value of the conscientious pursuit of excellence resides in its ability to reveal and exploit man's true potential."[7] Although he concedes that not everyone can attain excellence as he defines it, he takes shelter in Etienne Gilson's view that, "In short the only sound policy for any democracy is to raise the average level of its people by cultivating the excellence of the best among its citizens."[8]

For Keating, excellence resides in winning. He dismisses people who share the Grantland Rice (". . . how you play the game") and Baron DeCoubertin (". . . not the victory but the fight, not to win but to fight well") view of sport as regarding it with ". . . a quasi-religious reverence."[9] Keating praises Adolph Rupp, Kentucky's "great" basketball coach, (one can only assume that Keating meant to say "excellent" basketball coach, as in his terms that would mean Rupp's teams won a lot of games) and is especially impressed with an article that Rupp penned. It summarized his own position on the importance of victory. The article was entitled "Defeat and Failure To Me Are Enemies." From this we can get the gist of his position, although it smacks of platonic idealism, realism, or at best reification.[10] A quote from former University of Iowa Director of Athletics, Forest Evashevski, on the subject of the Rice/DeCoubertin position gives Keating more fuel for his fire. "You may as well say of a surgeon . . . that it matters not whether the patient lives or dies but how he makes the cut."[11] However, we might well accuse Evashevski of regarding sport and athletics with quasi-religious reverence of his own by equating them with a life or death situation in surgery.

Other allies in Keating's cause include former Army Head Football Coach, Colonel Earl Blaik who states, "The purpose of the game of football is to win, and to dilute the will to win is to destroy the purpose of football."[12] He also refers to Woody Hayes, ". . . a coach does not set out to build character, he goes out to win. The character will take care of itself."[13] The final ally Keating can muster is in the predictable form of the Tatum/Lombardi contention that, "Winning isn't the most important thing, it's the only thing."[14] Keating seems to imply that learning to win will build character, rather than destroy its last vestige.

From this position Keating proceeds to state that we are discussing two different types of activity here, sport and athletics. He claims that concern with sport "minimizes the importance of winning by insisting that there are other objects of equal or superior importance." While those concerned with athletics "believe that victory is the primary or exclusive goal,. . . and that *the values to be derived from such activity stem from the pursuit or attainment of victory*."[15] (My emphasis.)

Keating traces this discrepancy to the casual, synonymous use of the words sport and athletics. By this notion Rice, DeCoubertin, and their soul mates are referring to sport, while the legion of coaches he quotes are giving their views from the perspective of athletics.[16]

Keating's position is rooted in his distinction between sport and athletics. He claims that athletes are trying to win, whereas sportsmen are merely concerned with recreation and participation. This may be true anecdotally, but it is not necessarily so. But Keating proceeds to state that as a result of this differing emphasis, athletes quest for excellence while sportsmen do not. Keating analyzes the semantic roots of the words "sport" and "athletics" to further his argument. He emphasizes the recreational nature of the root of sport, "disport" and "disporter," which mean to "carry away." He then pounces on the origin of "athletics" and "athlete" in the Greek *"athlos"* and *"athlon"* which mean "contest" and "prize."[17]

From this perspective Keating claims support for his contention that the athlete is concerned with winning the contest to get the prize. In contrast, the sportsman is concerned with being carried away from the pressure of the everyday in a recreational activity. The conclusion is that sport and athletics are radically different types of human activity. The one a release or diversion, the other a quest for excellence through victory in the contest. He suggests that the Rice/DeCoubertin position is compatible with sport, but not athletics. As athletics by its nature tends towards the professional, Keating deduces that amateurism is the spirit of sport as he sees it

The Concepts of Play, Games, Sports, and Athletics

We need to examine more deeply the meaning of the terms play, games, sports, and athletics. The evolution of these concepts, in no small way, reflects post-Enlightenment thought, and as such helps to explain how the position represented by Keating came to be so influential.

In the relatively new field of sport philosophy, one of the first problematic areas was the definition of the area of concern. Today there is still no clear concensus on the limits and meanings of many of the terms used in sport philosophy.[18] In fact, a significant and influential faction of sport philosophers believe that this task is no longer worthwhile and is in fact, a barren enterprise. However, the course of this narrative now demands that we enter this arena.

In an attempt to define and contextualize sport, many writers begin with the concept of play because there is not only an apparent underlying play element in sport, but also because play has been the subject of scholarly attention for a considerable period of time.[19]

Play: When viewed as an activity, play is usually contrasted with work. Work is usually characterized by terms such as utilitarian, productive, serious, and it is very often not voluntary. By contrast,

Roger Caillois[20] states that play is marked by a number of character-istics. Play is voluntary, a person cannot be forced to play. Play has fixed and defined spatial and temporal limits, making it separate from the everyday world. It has conventions that supersede ordinary laws for the duration of the temporal and spatial limits. The outcome and incidents of play are not predetermined so it is marked by an element of uncertainty. Play has a fictive element and is free from the demands of productivity.

This characterization indicates that play is a complex conceptual construct and can hardly be conceived simply as non-work. There are many theoretical explanations of why we play. Carolyn Thomas examines thirteen of them under the headings of classic, recent, and modern theories of play. It is worth mentioning them at this point as they are representative of the post-Enlightenment desire to explain all phenomena in scientific terms. These theories are examples of the social sciences' attempts to predict and explain human behavior. Included under the heading of classic theories are: the Surplus Energy Theory, the Instinct Theory, the Preparation Theory, the Recapitula-tion Theory, and the Relaxation Theory.[21]

None of these theories offers an entirely satisfactory account of what play is or why we play, although some do offer partial accounts. They have not reached below the surface to the real nature of play. The ideas Thomas discusses under the heading of recent theories reflect the classic theories already mentioned but in varying degrees of refinement. The generalization-compensation theory views adult play as repeating generalized pleasant aspects of work and compensating for pleasures missing from work. In contrast, catharsis theory ex-plains play as a method of releasing aggression.

Under Thomas' modern theory classification, the psychoanalytic theory explains play as the role play of real life situations in a different context. Thus play, although motivated by the pleasure principle, aids the need to grow up and take an active role. This theory's support for the idea of a change of context once again shows a partial truth, but the notion that play is limited to real life situations limits its nature too much. Piaget's development theory views play as taking place in the mind of the child and then being physically expressed. As the intellect develops, the play becomes more structured and loses spon-taneity in adult sophistication. Less than explanations of play, these theories seem to reflect effects, results, and incomplete observations of play. In our western culture play was held in contempt under the protestant work ethic. Even today play is often seen as a second class activity, "mere play".

Gregory Bateson is nearer the heart of play when he refers to play as metacommunication, which is communication about communication. When playing we tell others by word, attitude or body posture, that what we are doing is not to be judged by the values of the everyday world. We are playing. If this is not made clear, and play is judged by the standards of the everyday, problems will follow. However, Bateson does not interpret play as license to do absolutely anything. Play has responsibilities to the safety of the player and others. Yet it is irresponsible, in as much as it needs no justification and is free from many of the restraints of everyday life.[22]

Games: John Loy defines games as ". . . any form of playful competition whose outcome is determined by physical skill, strategy, or chance, employed singly or in combination."[23] This is a worthy effort but makes the error of assuming that all games are contests. It would seem that Cailloie's play characteristics better describe games, i.e., a game is an activity separated from the ordinary by temporal and spatial restrictions, and regulated by separated rules, economically unproductive, uncertain in outcome, and fictive in nature. Guttman suggests a close link between play and games in his claim that games are organized play.[24] With this close relationship established, one can see more clearly why all games are not contests. For example, Guttman contrasts "leap frog" with basketball, and states that although both appear to meet the game criteria, basketball is a contest, it is more than a game. (Basketball fans have naturally long held this view.) Children's games, like "house," have rules and altered constraints of space and time, and most certainly are fictive in nature, yet there is no winner: the game is not a contest.

Sport and Athletics: The tendency in sport philosophy has been to take "games" as the form of activity, and to use sport and athletics to describe the meaning and intention of the activity. This is the case with Keating's view. For him sport becomes the name given to games played for recreation and distraction from the everyday. Athletics, on the other hand, is the name given to games played with winning as the only goal, all other benefits being dependent upon the victory.

Guttman[25] follows this trend but defines games that are physical contests as sport. He holds play and games as ends in themselves but takes sport as a contest where the object is to win. Clearly Keating would dispute this idea and claim that Guttmann confused sport with athletics. Harold Vanderzwaag makes a lucid distinction between sport and athletics that makes a slight adjustment to Keating's position. While Vanderzwaag also views athletics as exhibiting more concern with winning than sport does, he goes onto state that

"Athletics is geared first and foremost to attracting and pleasing spectators."[26] This idea is important in light of the discussions in the previous chapter. Keating's view of athletic excellence lends credence to those who would justify the exploitation and violence of contemporary sport in the name of the pursuit of excellence. This becomes inescapable once excellence is equated solely with victory in the contest.

It would seem that many of the views discussed so far address the nature of play, games, sports, and athletics with an unstated preconception to which category certain activities belong. They then "reason" their way into a justification for their own preconceptions: what Plato might call sophists, or Rorty, lovers of self-deceptive rhetoric. In common usage, sport is interchangeable with athletics. (It is interesting to note that in Great Britain athletics means what Americans call track and field and the term athlete will usually only be applied to a track and field competitor.) All sport and athletics is viewed as being a form of 'game' that we 'play'. The vocabulary is jumbled and mixed, with slack usage adding to the confusion.

It is against this background that Keating is able to produce a forceful semantic argument which claims to 'prove' that sport is recreational while athletics are combative. While it may be true that the term athletics has its origin in contesting for prizes, this does not necessarily justify the conclusion that the very essence of the athletic endeavor lies in "the pursuit of excellence through victory in the contest."

Despite his apparent semantic thoroughness, Keating fails to analyze the origins of the words "contest" and "competition," which he uses so freely and apparently thoughtlessly. "Competition" has its root in "competito," meaning to question or strive together.[27] "Contest" means to test together. Not to test against each other, but against the activity. Clearly competitors are partners in the test, needing and driving each other to greater heights: more like dance partners than adversaries. The contest drives all competitors to-wards excellence; it is not the sole possession of the winner alone, as the prize might be. In ancient Greece, the athletes were awarded prizes because they were excellent, they were not excellent because they won prizes.[28] Excellence must be attainable without necessarily winning the contest. Victory is too temporal and fickle a circumstance to equate it necessarily with excellence. Obviously one can win a contest without being excellent. The victor in a contest between two belligerent incompetents will not necessarily exhibit excellence. Whereas, the loser in a skilled and well-matched contest is not exempt from the possibility of displaying excellence. (For example, consider the image of a Soviet hockey team that loses to an NHL team, the Soviets are still excellent hockey players.) With this idea in mind, let us now return our attention to the concept of play and examine an alternative view that provides a basis for a concept of excellence other than victory in the contest.

Play: An Alternative View

Play is more than a process or activity. It can pervade nearly all activities at some level, but it cannot be grasped satisfactorily by the study of its outward appearance in the form of games, or from its effects as explained in psychological theory. Play can be found only in the player. It is a stance, a way of being in the world. Play is separate from the everyday world, but part of the real world, because play is real and has its own seriousness. Klaus Meier captures the spirit of play:

> "Play is heralded as an opportunity, and a forum, for man to experience, and to luxuriate in the pursuit of possibilities outside of everyday concerns and contexts, and relatively unconstrained by external intervention."[29]

Hyland interprets play as "a stance of responsive openness."[30] Play demands a heightened sense of openness to the environment, more than the non-play situation. This combined with a willingness to respond to the experience of openness produces the stance of play. Hyland suggests that this stance is reflected in "Socratic rationality,"[31] which requires the willingness to hold one's views and oneself open to question. Irrationality in Socratic terms is thus to fail to hold oneself open, resulting in closedness and fanaticism. This concept of rationality clearly conflicts with the rational thought that came to prominence after the Enlightenment. Post-Enlightenment rationality is synomymous with efficient means to arbitrarily chosen ends, a position in which concerns of efficiency and effectiveness outweigh consideration of reasonableness and fairness.

Hyland takes the stance of responsive openness to be grounded in a number of dualities, the most significant of which is our nature as incomplete and overfull, from which the other dualities spring. They are the tension between our nature as monadic and relational, and submission and dominance. The first duality, incomplete/overfull, is drawn largely from the work of Plato in the *Symposium*, and his concept of the nature of eros.

In the *Symposium*, the character of Aristophanes makes the case for our incomplete nature in which eros is our drive to overcome that state. The character of Aristophanes explains our questing for love as sexual joining to become complete again. He explains our situation by telling a story of how we were once double beings, but we aspired to be gods, so the gods split us into our present single forms. Those who were formerly of a male/female double are now heterosexual; those who were double males are now homosexual men; and, those who were double females are now lesbians. Thus, we all feel an incompleteness, but tragically, the whole we seek is flawed as well since we aspired to be gods.[32]

Plato identifies three important moments in the condition of incompleteness. First we *are* incomplete. Second, we recognize our incompleteness. Finally, we act to overcome the incompleteness. From this position, Plato states that the three part nature of eros does not only apply to sexual desire but to all forms of erotic desire. It applies to all attempts to overcome incompleteness, for example, the Platonic model of education fits this mold exactly.[33]

However, this is only half the story of the *Symposium*, for as the mother of eros is want, giving incompleteness, the father of eros is plenty. The paternal heritage is the root of our erotic nature as overfull. The overfullness is the source of our resourcefulness, power of activity, and creativity, which fires our creation of children, laws, poems, and works of art. Hyland claims that the dynamic tension between our nature as incomplete/overfull is one of the characteristics of play as a stance of responsive openness.[34]

It is now easy to see how the other two dualities, monadic/rational and submissive/dominant, arise from the first. The desire for completeness makes us relational; it is through relationships that we seek completeness. Yet our own specific manifestations of our erotic nature make us unique and thus monadic. Similarly our incompleteness makes us submissive, and we submit to the demands that we feel for completeness. But we have the power, our nature as overfull, to respond to our incompleteness. We can take a dominant stance as we luxuriate in our powers to achieve and forget our incompleteness. There is then a tension between dominance and submission that is a duality upon which Hyland bases the stance of play.[35]

Hyland claims that the stance of responsive openness is grounded in our nature as erotic, and that this is a teleological grounding.

"Because of our erotic nature, responsive openness becomes not merely descriptive of what we are but a desideratum."[36] To be responsively open is then to fulfill the telos of human being. Two important points arise from the fact that responsive openness is manifested as play. First, it is our nature as erotic, incomplete, yet overfull, to play. Second, play fulfills the telos of human being, one of the best and most human of possibilities.[37]

Hyland states that, "what Schiller says is true, we are most truly human—in the teleolgical sense—when we play."[38] Play then can be taken not just as a possible human stance, but as the most human stance, a view that has great consequences for the questions of value and excellence in athletics and life.

From this position the dichotomy of Keating vs. Rice/ DeCoubertin, or positivism vs. transcendentalism, can be re-addressed with play as a central theme. It could be held that if play is a stance it may, or may not, be part of the athletic occurrence, depending on the stance of the athletes. That is to say, play may be manifested in athletics without being a necessary part of it. This view holds that the damage to games and sports is already done in athletics by its very nature; a spectacle with no necessary play element. Or it may be contended that there is a necessary play element to athletics, and if an athlete does not have a stance of responsive openness, then the integrity of the situation is violated. In this case, the activity can no longer legitimately be called athletics, any more than gladiatorial combat was athletics in ancient Rome. This view requires a play element in athletics or it ceases to be athletics, and becomes mere spectacle, bereft of moral content, valued for its crowd pleasing and money making effects, and ceases to be essentially humane or humanizing.

An Escape From Keating; Winning is not Necessarily Excellence

In the wake of the re-examination of play, Keating's position must be questioned. He starts his diatribe from the Homeric hero, the heroes in the epics the *Iliad* and *Odyssey*. These works are indeed the main source of information on sport from that time period. As a result, contemporary scholars have analyzed the contents of these works with predictably conflicting conclusions. For example, Allan Stull and Guy Lewis concur with Keating, claiming that the Greeks were obsessed with winning as a symbol of excellence and equate the concept of *arete* with being the best at something.[39] By contrast the revisionist scholarship of Matthew Dickie is neared the heart of the matter in his examination of the funeral games in the *Iliad*. He concludes that although winning was undoubtedly important, it was not overridingly so, and conversely, defeat was no disgrace in itself.[40] Dickie is closer to the concept of Greek arete. Arete has been translated into English as virtue, excellence, and quality. In human beings the concept is often asssociated with rational behavior, but it also has undertones of efficiency and effectiveness in action. It is opposed in Greek by the concept of hubris, a state of overbearing pride, arrogance, or insolence—in other words, overstepping your mark and making a fool of yourself. This was the state to be avoided. For instance, a Homeric Bobby Knight would be the subject of universal scorn, an embarrassment to himself and his city and certainly not the recipient of great accolades and honors. In this context, sport provided an opportunity to show one's quality as a person, and not just by winning. The Greek sought to be just in victory, gracious in defeat, but always heroic in the striving.

MacIntyre makes an interesting observation on the significance of the works of Homer to his own time.

> What the poet of the *Iliad* sees, and his characters do not, is that winning too may be a form of losing. For Achilles in his moment of reconciliation with Priam has no way of represent-ing to himself what Homer is able in his account of Achilles and Priam to represent to others. Thus the *Iliad* puts in question what neither Achilles nor Hector can put into question; the poem lay claim to a form of understanding which it denies to those whose actions it describes.[41]

This suggests that the relevance of the heroes lies not in their deeds and values, but in the illustrations of values their interaction demonstrates. So it would seem a very naive interpretation of Homer to admire the heroes for themselves, as Keating does, rather than for their part in illuminating the narrative scheme.

The concept of arete as excellence offers an alternative to Keating's concept of excellence. He is careful to define the term as being the best, regardless of flaws one may have as a person. Once we accept this position his logic carries us soundly through to his conclusions. In the equating of winning with excellence, and excellence with winning, Keating has produced a condition that Christopher Lasch described in his *Culture of Narcissisum*.[42] Achievement has no reference point except to itself: success is to succeed. The consequences of such an existence can be seen in the rhetoric of competition in society as a whole. The free market distribution of all commodities and services results ultimately in the rich having possibilities denied to the poor. Some might say that this is a fair system. However, it may be fair to determine which type of automobile one drives in this way, but it is certainly not a just way to distribute life saving medical technology. Just as there is a need to humanize this problem, so there is also a need to humanize Keating's concept of excellence in athletics.

Human existence resides in being an excellent human. To achieve any goal at the expense of the denial of the importance of human excellence is to cease to be humane. Hyland might say that excellence in athletics lies in the fulfillment of the human telos in responsive openness. Keating's claim that the value of the "Conscious pursuit of excellence resides in its ability to reveal and exploit man's true potential,"[43] gives the game away. Keating seeks to exploit the potential in man, but to what end? The end of more excellence, or more winning? To the Gilson end of raising the average level of the members of society?[44] How can these human resources be exploited in a humane way? How will the average rise in the level of the members be detected without reducing them all to statistics?

Keating would evade my objections by falling back on his distinction between sport and athletics. He claims that the two are totally different types of activity, and the objectors to his concept of athletics are really proponents of sport who do not understand the distinction.

> One group minimizes the importance of winning by insisting that there are objects of equal or superior importance. The others believe that victory is the primary or exclusive goal . . . and that the values to be derived from such activities stem from the pursuit or attainment of victory.[45]

This statement is problematic because to claim that winning is not the primary value of athletics is not to "minimize" the importance of winning; it is to contextualize it. The notion that "the other values" can be achieved as incidentals to the pursuit or attainment of victory also presents problems. Doing what it takes to win is being presented as an educational and valid experience in itself. Keating offers a philosophical justification for the objectified values of post-Enlightenment society being applied to athletics. The clear-cut and scientific analysis of human athletic performance is thus provided by the objective assessment of the scoreboard. This position is what Nietzsche described, predicted, and feared would be the fate of every aspect of our lives: namely, the naked power struggle where power is its own justification in a war of all against all.

Summary

Keating describes athletics as an activity devoted to winning, and this victory is the contest he equates with excellence. He very deliberately points out that excellence requires no worthiness of the individual. His effort to recruit the support of the Homeric hero as well as the modern sport heroes is an ill-fated attempt to unify the past and present to justify his own views. Keating is a product of modern culture, his reason is not that of Plato but the instrumental reason of the post-Enlightenment world. His analysis works from activity types and makes a justification of the rational and instrumental values of modernity. This is a world where winning is excellence because there are no other rationally and logically demonstrated values. Winning is the distillation of excellence in this world, as power is authority. Sport cannot be a separate realm, the values of sport are the values of society.

Keating misses the root of sport and athletics in play. Play as responsive openness can be present in all activities, it is not defined by activities or activity types. If athletics is nothing but a fight for a prize, then it is a spectacle and dehumanizing. As such, athletics would not be an arena in which excellence would have any meaning. If the heart of athletics is still play, there is more to it than winning. The stance of responsive openness, grounded in our erotic nature, the dualities of incomplete/overfull, dominant/submissive and relational/monadic, introduces a depth and meaning that goes far beyond winning as the test of excellence. It is the relationship of the craftsman to his skill and the artist to his vision.

This ends Part One of the study, the analysis and critique of the culture that values results over performance. The development of contemporary society from the revolutionary ideas of the Enlightenment was addressed in chapter 1. The emergence of modern sport and the effects of contemporary values in sport were addressed in chapter 2. Finally, here in chapter 3, the consequences of these developments in the equating of excellence with winning were examined.

Part Two of the study examines the possibilities of forming a different basis for valuing athletic performance. The contemporary world is based on radical individualism, which has destroyed all values save for objective and instrumental ones. In a world where absolute and universal values are no longer held to exist, it is only through shared values that order can exist in any form but oppression of the weak by the powerful. Values in sport and society need to be based on a community that is more than a loose alliance of consumers and exploiters torn by the currents of market forces.

PART TWO

The Game is How You Play it

CHAPTER 4

Contemporary Community: A Way Back?

Thus far this study has examined the consequences of Enlightenment thought culminating in contemporary society. The effects of the cultural values of contemporary society on the development of modern sport have been examined, and the philosophical consequences for sport, distilled in the equating of excellence with winning, has been addressed. The task of this work now turns from description to synthesis as I intend to establish a basis upon which to stand in the shifting sands of contemporary society where, in the words of Karl Marx, "all that is solid melts into air." Such a position must provide an alternative to the objectification of the post-Enlightenment world so that the valuing of performances, and not just results, might be explained and supported.

In *After Virtue*, Alasdair MacIntyre provides an excellent basis, a framework of social concepts, that could support a society with alternative concepts of value. However, his work is based on a return to an Aristotelian world, which is problematic in itself. MacIntyre's position will be discussed in depth and critiqued with a view to accepting the social framework but rejecting the Aristotelianism.

Balanced against MacIntyre's Aristotelian interpretation is a Nietzschean interpretation that MacIntyre rejects but that I accept. The exploration of MacIntyre's framework and the examination of Nietzsche's work are critical to this narrative. MacIntyre's concepts of a practice, the narrative unity of a life, and a tradition, all speak directly to the contemporary sport world and offer insights into its condition. In trying to overcome the valuing of results over performance, the social framework provided by MacIntyre offers powerful possibilities.

Sports can be viewed as practices and as such, have internal value and excellences more rich and complex than can be expressed when excellence is simply equated with winning. Why then is Nietzsche important? MacIntyre bases his position on accepting something like Aristotle's concept of the virtues, and further claims that if Aristotle is rejected, as he was by post-Enlightenment philosophers, the alternative must be the horrors of a Nietzschean world. My claim is that not only does MacIntyre's framework provide a basis for understanding values in sport beyond winning, but that we can reject Aristotle and find a Nietzschean world that is not necessarily horrendous.

This narrative now demands that we examine the work of the greatest critic of modernity, Friedrich Nietzsche. The power of his position, the pervasiveness of his work, the misinterpretation of his philosophy, and the implications of his work for man, all demand careful examination at this point.

The Power of Nietzsche's Position

Nietzsche, like all prophets, was not recognized by his own people in his own time. His works were virtually unread in Germany until after his death, or at least his intellectual demise. Nietzsche has been misinterpreted and maligned, a fate he predicted for himself. His work foretold of the condition of the western world with the death of God, whether in the form of the Judeo-Christian God, or absolute and universal truth, both of whom expired at the hands of the Enlightenment mob. Nietzsche described himself as a destiny, a man after whom nothing would be the same.[1]

Nietzsche wrote consistently, or at least continually, on several recurring themes. All of these can be traced to the apocalypse of the death of God, and/or the structure of values created by man to fill the resulting void. In his earliest work, *The Birth of Tragedy*, Nietzsche examines the cultural values of the ancient Athenians. He described ancient Athens as a society in which the opposing forces of the Dionysian and the Apollinian were locked in a powerful embrace: not a lover's caress but a warrior's salute. The Apollinian represented the genius of restraint, harmony and measure, while the Dionysian represented the excesses and drunken frenzy of the festival and music. Nietzsche makes the point that one cannot truly understand Greek art without grasping first the enormous price the Greeks paid for their art.[2] The price was paid in the form of the huge efforts needed to harness the Dionysian powers, and channel them into the production of such art. The titanic struggle gave birth to the Greek tragedy, which Nietzsche claims is the imposition on the Dionysian of the

Apollinian. Nietzsche admires the Greeks for creating such tragedies, in which they affirm the beautiful despite the reality of human existence. This is a function that might well be attributed to contemporary sport, a form of tragic theatre.[3]

Nietzsche was an opponent of Plato for his excessive rationality. Plato opposed the poets, writers of tragedy, because they presented an untrue picture of an illusionary world. They did not give insight into reality, but subjective expression of their subjective existence. Furthermore, tragedy portrays virtues in conflict, a concept totally unacceptable in Plato's scheme of ideal forms. To Nietzsche, Plato opposed the only real way to understand human beings, that is, through art and not science.

Nietzsche portrays the Athenian Greeks as a force before which we feel fear and inadequacy. He sees them as the chariot drivers of every subsequent culture but the ". . . chariots and horses are of too poor a quality for the drivers, who then make sport of driving the chariot into the abyss—which they themselves clear with the bold leap of Achilles."[4]

For Nietzsche, Socrates is one of these charioteers, the first of a new type of "theoretical man." A man Nietzsche directly contrasts with the artist,

> . . . the artist having unveiled the truth garment by garment, remains with his gaze fixed on what is still hidden, theoretical man takes delight in the cast garments and finds his highest satisfaction in the unveiling process itself, which proves to him his own power.[5]

This characterization of the rational scientific position illustrates Nietzsche's rejection of the scientific quest for absolute truth; a quest he sees as quite futile. So much so that he praises Gotthold Lessing (most honest of theoretical men) for daring ". . . to say that the search for truth was more important to him than truth itself and thereby revealed the innermost secrets of inquiry, to the surprise and annoyance of his fellows."[6] Nietzsche continues:

> Yet, sure enough, alongside sporadic perception such as this one of Lessing's, which represented an act of honesty as well as highspirited defiance, we find a type of deep seated illusion, first manifested in Socrates: the illusion that thought, guided by the thread of causation, might plumb the farthest abysses of being and even correct it. This grand metaphysical illusion has become integral to the scientific endeavor and again and again leads science to those far limits of its inquiry where it becomes art.[7]

To Nietzsche, science was claiming power and insight where art was the real method. The metaphysical illusion is that rational thought can explain and even correct the irrational existence of man.

Socrates was not only the first man to live by the rules of rational inquiry, but also the first man to die by them. As Plato documents in the *Apology*, Socrates is freed from the fear of death by his powers of reason.[8] This emblem, which Nietzsche claims ". . . hangs above the portal of every science reminds the adept that his mission is to make existence appear intelligible and thereby justified."[9]

Nietzsche would claim that the pre-Socratic Athenians were Greece's greatest flowering and that Socrates signaled the beginning of the end of Greek culture. In a way this is clearly an accurate assessment as the Greek Enlightenment preceded the collapse into Roman domination. The concomitant rise of the importance of the individual is usually charged with causing the decline of ancient Greece, but it was the philosophy of Socrates that placed the individual in a central position and his concept of the power of reason that gave the individual the weapon to further his own cause. This is, of course, the root of the conflict of Socrates with the Sophists. Socrates wanted to use reason to recall the ideal forms; the Sophists used reason for practical secular ends because they denied the existence of the ideal forms: they were relativists. The Greek Enlightenment saw a similar absolutist/relativist confrontation as that central to the Enlightenment itself, nearly two thousand years later.

Nietzsche held art to be the true mode of human expression and knowledge, and not science with its reason and reductions. To Nietzsche our need was for a kind of poetic Socrates, a Friedrich Nietzsche.

The Pervasiveness of Nietzsche's Insight

In modern post-Enlightenment culture, Nietzsche saw the death of God and the loss of all values. It should be remembered that Nietzsche was no admirer of Judeo-Christian morals, but that he still realized the consequences of the loss of those values.[10] The excessive use of reason in Socrates' time, and that which exploded in sixteenth century Europe, had always been oppressed by religious belief. But in the Enlightenment, reason overcame this opposition to all practical and political ends. Nietzsche proclaimed the death of God, and foresaw the consequences, totalitarianism, the loss of the root of all values, and life without guidance at the mercy of the merciless.

Nietzsche postulated the existence of "the will to power," which he found in all kinds of human behavior and values. He proclaimed this as man's basic motivational force. The power in question can be characterized in self-control, art, and philosophy. A man who has this power will be self-possessed and fear no man, nor even death. Unlike Socrates, who was freed from the fear of death by reason, the man of power is freed from this fear by virtue of his own vitality. He is freed not by rationality but by irrational forces.[11]

A correlative of the will to power to which Nietzsche often returns in his writing is the concept of "resentment." This is a feeling of under-privilege stemming from a dirth of experience. This term is rich and textured and has connotations of unjustified dissatisfaction at being excluded, or feeling that a right to something exists when it does not.[12] This concept is allied to that of the "slave morality" which opposes good and evil, and the "master morality" which opposes good and bad. For Nietzsche, the slave morality stresses evil with good in a supporting role, while the master morality stresses good with bad in a supporting role. So the resentful man of the slave morality feels his exclusion is evil, while the man of power, the man of the master morality, looks to the good that exists even if it is not his own.[13]

The man of power is described as the "overman," able to define and create himself in the world without God. The overman describes himself in his own terms and does not allow others to determine his being by their description of him. He creates himself by the creation of his own values, and creates his own reality in the process. The mark of the overman is that his creation is so strong that others will take his reality as their own. Examples are easily found in sport, individuals who have created their own reality for others. Muhammad Ali is a good example from profes-sional boxing, Julius Erving in professional basketball, O.J. Simpson in professional football, and Wayne Gretsky in professional hockey: all did more than excel, they re-defined their sport.

The overman creates his own standards and affirms life even in the face of the terrors of human existence. A tragic hero? Certainly a tragic figure but one who feels no resentment. With no external objective and absolute truth for guidance in post-Enlightenment society, the overman is the man who can still act as if there were some meaning to life, although he knows there is not. He creates his own values and meaning without claiming them to be more than that. This is what Alexander Nehamus calls Nietzschean perspectivism, the willingness to see one's own position as simply that: one's own position, one among many possible alternative views.[14] But the mean-ing the overman creates has some surpassing dignity that others lack. The overman is not one who thinks himself superior in some petulant way, but one who drives himself hard, sets difficult goals for himself, and demands more of himself than of others.

The Misinterpretation of Nietzsche's Work

These main themes of Nietzsche's work, the death of God, the will to power, and the concept of the overman, have all been radically misinterpreted over the years. The result has been much unjustified criticism of both Nietzsche and his work. This is partly due to Nietzsche's style of writing, a very literary genre, demanding careful attention and reflection from the reader. It is indeed ironic that Nietzsche and Aristotle are even opposed in writing style, Aristotle gives us lecture notes, while Nietzsche gives us poetry.

Nietzsche did not celebrate the death of God as a committed atheist would. Rather, he announces the death of God and is horrified by the consequences he saw as a result. The concepts of the will to power and the overman were examples of how we might retain some cultural values. Motivated by the will to power, the overman could rise from the desolation of modernity and the mob to champion humanity. These were not idealizations but consequences of modernity. They tell us that if anything is to remain that is worthwhile, it will take the use of power to preserve it. The power over ourselves.

However, a vulgar reading of the will to power and the overman makes these concepts seem like a justification of an exceedingly competitive and selfish society, a collection of individuals pursuing their own unenlightened interests. Nietzsche can then be interpreted as condoning power politics and the triumph of the powerful over the powerless. These ideas were combined with a racist interpretation in the perversion of Nietzsche's work carried out by the Nazi Party of Adolph Hitler. It is only relatively recently that Nietzsche has been exhumed from his fascist tomb and resurrected as the authentic creative force that he does represent.[15]

The Implications of Nietzsche's Position

The idea that the will to power motivates us all is not a moral judgment, it is not necessarily good or bad. Nietzsche neither praises nor blames it, but acknowledges it. The will to power makes the overman. He is self-possessed, sets his own standards for himself, not for others and does not seek to impose them on others, although they may adopt them. This is the Nietzschean existential man, the tragic hero, creating and living his own existence.

The overman could not be a political leader, according to Nietzsche. He is a self-leader. The mob of democracy would only pollute his ideas and the dictatorship of fascism choke the individual.

"The party man necessarily becomes a liar."[16] Nietzsche bewails the coming times, our time, when he says of "the children of the future":

> We "conserve" nothing; neither do we want to return to any past periods; we are not by any means "liberal"; we do not work for "progress"; we do not plug our ears against the sirens who in the market place sing of the future; their song about "equal rights," "free market society," "no more masters and no more servants" has no allure for us. We simply do not consider it desirable that a realm of justice and concord should be established on earth; we are delighted with all who love, as we do, danger, war, and adventure, who refuse to compromise; to be captured, reconciled, and castrated; we count ourselves among conquerors; we think about the necessity for new orders, also for a new slavery—for every strengthening and enhancement of the human type also involves a new enslavement.[17]

The overman is a creative force, not a creature, who creates his own destiny, his own end, independently of others. Nietzsche speaks of the children of tomorrow as being in opposition to the politics and society of the day, yet unable to escape to the realm of the overman because each new social movement is its own kind of restriction. The overman makes his own order. Nietzsche's overman is essentially singular because his authentic existential nature would be compromised by the inauthentic nature of political and social life. The tragedy of the overman is that he knows the depth of the abyss beneath him, yet he lives as if it were not there, as if life had meaning and purpose. The overman lives by the authentic values he creates for himself and faces the consequences.

This sketch of the Nietzschean position was necessary before we examine MacIntyre's thesis from *After Virture* in order that it is clear to what MacIntyre is trying to provide an alternative. However, in his desire to avoid what he sees as the necessarily evil Nietzschean view, he accepts a value system based on a society of privilege, where values are clear because they are part of the structure of society, or in Aristotle's case, the city state. It is my contention that the framework MacIntyre creates is not essentially Aristotelian, and that Nietzscheanism can work within it just as well, if not better. Furthermore, the Aristotelian aspects of MacIntyre's work make it unacceptable in the post-Enlightenment world.

MacIntyre's View: The Refutation of Nietzsche

Alasdair MacIntyre's thesis in *After Virtue* hinges on being able to show that Nietzsche does not have the final word on modern life. To do this he tries to achieve two goals. First, he tries to show that the Enlightenment was mistaken to totally reject Aristotle, and that "something like the virtues according to Aristotle" are not only feasible but necessary for contemporary community. Then MacIntyre tries to discredit Nietzsche's position.

MacIntyre opposes Aristotle and Nietzsche in a dramatic either/or situation. Either we resurrect Aristotle's thought, or we are doomed to the Nietzschean world, which MacIntyre sees as necessarily horrendous. MacIntyre takes Nietzsche to be the spokesman or prophet of the most extreme liberal individualism. Not an advocate or true believer, but someone who faced the consequences of the Enlightenment more squarely than anyone before him. As such, MacIntyre does not deny the power of Nietzsche's work. In fact, it is the great achievements of Nietzsche that make him so central a figure in MacIntyre's thesis.

For it was Nietzsche's historic achievement to understand more clearly than any other philosopher—certainly more clearly than his counterparts in Anglo-Saxon emotivism and continental existentialism—not only that what purported to be appeals to objectivity were in fact expressions of subjective will, but also the nature of the problem that this posed for philosophy.

> In a famous passage in *The Gay Science* (section 335) Nietzsche jeers at the notion of basing morality on inner moral sentiments, on conscience, on the one hand, or on the Kantian categorical imperative, on the other. In five swift, witty and cogent paragraphs he disposes of both what I have called the Enlightenment project to discover rational foundations for an objective morality and for the confidence of the everyday moral agent in post-Enlightenment culture that his moral practice and utterance are in good order.[18]

Nietzsche is MacIntyre's Achilles, shattering the ranks of the Enlightenment philosophers, but, like Achilles, Nietzsche is denied his due, as MacIntyre takes his victory as proof that the Enlightenment embodied a fatal error. Richard Bernstein is correct in his observation on this pivotal issue in the MacIntyre thesis that the alternative he posed ". . . is not just one view of morality versus another—it is, rather, morality versus no morality."[19]

This is just how MacIntyre frames the issue. The choice is not between Aristotle and Nietzsche, there is no such choice. Rather, if we were right to reject the Aristotilian virtues embodied in pre-sixteenth century culture, then the failure of the Enlightenment thinkers to produce a rational basis for morality leaves the Nietzschean world as the inescapable consequences. If Nietzsche wins, he wins by default.[20]

MacIntyre claims that the rejection of Aristotle's concept of the virtues was in fact a mistake. Furthermore, MacIntyre proposes an interpretation of the virtues according to Aristotle, which he claims provides a grounded position from which the failings of Nietzsche's perspective can be clearly seen.[21]

MacIntyre talks of "something like" Aristotle's account of the virtues because he acknowledges some failings in Aristotle's work. In fact, there are three major aspects of Aristotle's view of the virtues that MacIntyre finds unacceptable. The first is the metaphysical biology that supports the class system and limited freedom within the city state. The second is the ahistorical nature of Aristotle's philosophy. The third is the rejection of the possibility of tragedy. Aristotle's conception of the virtues left no room for the possibility of different conflicting virtues; they are a harmonious whole. In its extreme, his view suggests that you cannot have one virtue without having them all.[22]

The problem MacIntyre faces is that of producing an Aristotelianism without city states. He is faced with the task of showing that his Aristotelian framework can hold up under the weight of the knowledge that the city state was not the final word on human society, but one stopping off point in the process of an unfolding and enfolding history. MacIntyre wants to develop a theory that preserves the Aristotelian virtues but escapes the inherent flaws.

The virtues are teleological to Aristotle. Their purpose is to enable "man-as-he-is" to become "man-as-he-could-be" if he realized his telos. The virtues enable man to pursue the good life, not as a social role, but the good life for man as such. Homeric virtues enabled men to perform their social roles. Thus, Homeric virtue had an external telos, and the virtues came from the social role. But for Aristotle, the social roles came from the virtues, and thus, from the good life for man.[23]

A further distinction can be drawn by introducing Benjamin Franklin's concept of the virtues. While Franklin did hold the virtues to be teleological, they were taken as the means to the end of happiness reflected in success and prosperity in Philadelphia, and later in heaven. In all three cases, that of Aristotle, Homer, and Franklin, the virtues are secondary to a social construct, respectively; the good life for man (telos), a social role, and utilitarian material gain.[24]

From these examples emerges the importance of the social construct, the conceptual background, against which the virtues are to be understood. MacIntyre offers three levels of social grounding for his concept of the virtues. The first is the concept of a "practice"; the second is the concept of "the narrative unity of a single life"; and the third is the concept of a tradition. Each stage presupposes the previous one, not vice-versa.[25] It is this framework which I wish to retain, but without the Aristotelian virtues to support it.

The Practice

The concept of a practice, according to MacIntyre, refers to,

> . . . any coherent and complex form of socially established coopera-
> tive human activity through which goods internal to that form of
> activity are realized in the course of trying to achieve those stan-
> dards of excellence which are appropriate to and partly definitive of,
> that form of activity, with the result that human powers to achieve
> excellence, and human conceptions of the ends and goods involved
> are systematically extended.[26]

The concept of a practice is distinct from techniques or skills related to a practice. For example, kicking a soccerball is not a practice, but the game of soccer is. Planting seeds is not a practice, but agriculture is. Conducting an experiment is not a practice, but the investigations of all sciences are, along with the practice of medicine, music, and art.

The social concept of a practice is very illuminating and useful in gaining insight into how athletics and the role of the athlete can be valued in some way other than by winning contests. The notion of standards of excellence internal to the practice is important as the practice is self referential. The goods that are made available through the practice are internal to the practice. The key component is that of "goods internal to the practice." These are goods that cannot be obtained in any other way but from that specific practice, and to obtain them one must be a practitioner. "Those who lack relevant experiences are incomplete thereby as judges of internal goods."[27]

It is the blindness to internal goods in sport that leads to the valuation of results over performance. There is a quality of experience that can only be obtained through the practice of specific sports; whereas external goods can be obtained through the trade of any commodity. The internal value of sport as a practice lies in the relationship of the athlete to the sport. Furthermore, the internal goods of soccer cannot be obtained through the practice of football, or basketball, and vice-versa, as the internal goods are unique and specific, not generic and general.

There is a distinction between internal and external goods that may or may not be conferred upon the practitioner. External goods are contingent upon some outside agency and could take the form of money, fame, and status. However, they are not internal aspects of the practice, they do not necessarily come from the practice, and could be achieved in other ways.

Characteristically external goods are the property of one individual and the more one person has the less there is for others. As a result, external goods are the subject of competition where there must be losers as well as winners. Internal goods are also the outcome of competition to excel, but it is characteristic of them that their achievement is a good for the whole community involved in the practice.[28]

MacIntyre claims that, "A virtue is an acquired human quality the possession and exercise of which tends to enable us to achieve those goods which are internal to practices and the lack of which effectively prevents us from achieving any such goods."[29]

This claim is premised by the assertion that a practice demands the practitioner subordinate himself to the authority of the standards and exponents of the practice. The practitioner must take his place in the practice as the history of the practice unfolds. The practitioner must learn what is due and to whom, make sacrifices and partake authentically in a critical dialogue.[30]

> In other words we have to accept as necessary components of any practice with internal goods and standards of excellence the virtues of justice, courage and honesty. For not to accept these . . . so far bars us from achieving the standards of excellence or the goods internal to the practice that it renders the practice pointless except as a device for achieving external goods.[31]

MacIntyre requires a relationship of a particular kind between the practitioners in order to preserve the integrity of the practice and thus internal goods. It is a virtuous relationship that is needed, but the vicious and meanspirited necessarily rely on the virtues of others within a practice for it to flourish. Furthermore, they deny themselves the experience of the internal good that the virtuous enjoy.[32]

The framework that the concept of a practice provides helps to explain some of the contradictions in contemporary sport. The athlete who is not rewarded by internal goods, and who violates the practice in his quest for external goods, is easier to understand and discuss within this framework. He is not doing wrong, rather he is missing out. There is also a correlation between the culture of personality, with its emphasis on appearance and image, and the accumulation of external goods. The internal goods are quiet and introspective, and quite invisible to those who do not share in them. Whereas the trappings of "success" in external goods are valued partly for their obviousness and covetability.

Institutions and Practices

Practices, MacIntyre points out, should not be confused with institutions. Football, medicine and golf are practices, but the Los Angeles Raiders, OSU Hospital, and St. Andrews are all institutions. Institutions are characteristically concerned with external goods. They are structured in terms of power, status, and money, acquiring more than they distribute as rewards. The institution has no notion of any internal good to the practice. However, no practice can survive long without the protection of a bureaucratic wing or institution. This relationship is such that the ideals and values of the practice are always vulnerable to the acquisitiveness and exploitation of the institution. The concern for common good within the practice is threatened by the competitiveness of the institution. The importance of the virtues, MacIntyre claims, is that "without them, without justice, courage and truthfulness, the practice could not resist the corrupting power of the institutions."[33]

To the practitioner, the practice is a source of internal good, preserved by the virtue of those involved. To the institution, the practice is a source of external goods, power, wealth, and status. To the institution, the practice should be managed to maximize the production of these goods. One could think of many examples of this dichotomy. For example, contrast the surgeon dedicated to the practice of medicine and the saving of human life with the hospital manager who has cashiers trying to collect payments from patients in the post-op rooms. Or similarly, the university department run on such bureaucratic lines that it has become managerially expedient not to serve the interests of the students, nor to aid its own practitioners. The sting in the tail of all this for the practitioners is that if his virtue fails him and he also uses the practice only for its external goods, then the practice will die. The practice will die a little every time a practitioner fails to maintain the practice in the face of institutions covetousness; but the institution will not even realize anything has happened. This is a common leverage point for institutions against authentic practitioners. Take the case of the university athletics director and the minor sport coach who wants more money for his program. The coach threatens to resign if the university will not finance his team to a competitive level. The AD tells him to go ahead and resign, and that will be the end of his program. It will be scrapped. The practice will die, but the institution will carry on with its other programs oblivious to the loss. The coach therefore carries on with insufficient funds, or kills his own practice.

Bernstein fails to grasp the relationship MacIntyre describes between internal goods and the virtues, and practices and institutions. This becomes apparent when he comments on the relationship of the virtues to practices that:

> ... in the case of chess, we may discover that in order to achieve its internal goods, one needs to cultivate one's powers of memory, concentration, abilities to anticipate possible strategies, etc. These then would be, according to MacIntyre's definition, the virtues required to excel in chess.[34]

Bernstein is here confusing internal goods with excelling in a practice and therefore confuses the virtues with what it takes to excel. It seems Bernstein is using the word 'excel' in a manner compatible with Keating's concept of excellence as winning or achieving. Bernstein goes onto make the following observation:

> Presumably we are living in a time when there has been a "decline" in the virtues. Yet, many of the practices that MacIntyre specifies thrive. But if practices cannot be sustained without truthfulness, justice, and courage, then the very existence of practices such as chess, farming, architecture, and enquires of physics, chemistry, and biology should count as evidence for the flourishing of the virtues.[35]

Bernstein is observing successful institutions and assuming that the practices they encapsulate are surviving intact. Simply because the NFL is flourishing it does not follow that the practice of football is even alive in that league. The NFL is an institution, and as such is blind to the internal goods available in the practice of football. Put another way, the creation and distribution of external goods does not indicate that internal goods are necessarily being created as well. The virtues are required, according to MacIntyre, to protect the internal goods of the practice from the corruption of the institution. The virtues do not result in any success within the practice; they are not instrumental to external goods, but to internal goods. As MacIntyre clearly states:

> Virtues then stand in a different relationship to external and to internal goods. The possession of the virtues—and not only of their

semblance and simulacra—is necessary to achieve the latter; yet the possession of the virtues may perfectly well hinder us in achieving the external goods.[36]

The virtues needed to achieve the internal standards of excellence in a practice are not technical skills, although these will be needed by the practitioner. The virtues required are something like those of *sophrosune* and *phronesis*. These are ancient virtues that refer respectively to not abusing one's position and knowing what is due to others. The internal goods of a practice are only accessible to the virtuous, not to the merely technically adept. The goods lie in the relationship of the practitioner to the practice and not solely in the achievement of high level performance. So it follows that MacIntyre can state:

> It is not part of my thesis that great violinists cannot be vicious or that great chess players mean-spirited. Where the virtues are required, the vices also may flourish. It is just that the vicious and mean-spirited necessarily rely on the virtues of others for the practices in which they engage to flourish and also deny themselves the experience of achieving those internal goods which may reward even not very good chess players and violinists.[37]

It can then be claimed that great athletes are not necessarily good people, and are not necessarily practitioners of the sport in which they dominate, but they rely on the virtue of others to keep the practice alive, while denying themselves the experience of the internal goods. Here MacIntyre is clearly stating that athletic excellence does not equate to victory in the contest, but that excellence resides in practicing the sport and partaking in the internal goods.

However, MacIntyre identifies three areas in which the practice alone proves unable to provide a basis for something like Aristotle's account of the virtues. First, the concept of the practice is so all embracing that "too many" conflicts with "too much" arbitrariness would result, and the internal goods then are based on personal preference.[38]

The second fault in the framework of the practices is that without an overriding conception of the 'telos' of a whole human life the account of the virtues remains incomplete. The third area MacIntyre points to is reinforced by the first two; the concept of the tradition, from which the virtue of constancy or integrity is recognized.[39]

The Narrative Order of a Single Human Life

MacIntyre is now faced with the task of building the case for the conception of a human life as a narrative unity within a tradition. In trying to present a contemporary version of, ". . . each human life as a whole, as a unity, whose character provides the virtues with an adequate telos," MacIntyre faces two different kinds of obstacles.[40] One is social and the other philosophical, but both are rooted in the consequences of modernity.

The social obstacle is derived from the way in which modern life is divided into separated realms, work/leisure, public/private, corporate/personal, also youth, middle age, and old age. Each segment has its own norms and modes of behavior, thus the distinctiveness of each area is emphasized and not the unity of the life of the individual who passes through those sections.

The philosophical obstacles arise from two distinctive tendencies, one mainly in analytic philosophy, the other in existentialism and social theory. The analytic problem is that of viewing human actions atomistically, the good Cartesian has been taught to break everything down to its simplest components. In this way, the most complex of relationships is reduced to simple explanations. The existential problem arises from the tendency to see the self as something totally separate from the roles that the individual plays. The sociological theory problem lies in the antithesis of the existential problem, that is to see the self as nothing more than the roles the individual plays.

MacIntyre suggests that the concept of the self, ". . . whose unity resides in the unity of a narrative which links birth to life to death as narrative beginning to middle to end,"[41] is not as unfamiliar as might be thought at first. All to the contrary, because of its historical importance in our past, the narrative concept of self has an unacknowledged presence in many of our thoughts and acts in the present.

Take the example of a man playing baseball. He could be described as preparing for spring: throwing and hitting, socializing, or taking exercise and pleasing his wife. If his primary intention is to prepare his game for spring then he is part of an annual cycle of social activity, part of a particular narrative history of course baseball. If on the other hand he was primarily taking exercise and pleasing his wife then he is part of a narrative history of a marriage, a different social setting. MacIntyre concludes from this type of example that we cannot ". . . characterize behavior independently of intentions," neither can we ". . . characterize intentions independently of the settings which make those intentions intelligible both to agents themselves and to others."[42]

The distillation of this position is that actions are identified by an inter-relationship of the intention, the setting, and the history of the agent. The intentions are placed in, ". . . causal and temporal order with reference to their role in his or her history."[43] They are also placed in relation to the history of the social setting to which they belong.

What distinguishes these concepts from social roles is that a role determines behavior, a narrative unity explains behavior and provides a way to judge it. The unity of an individual life, according to MacIntyre, consists in the unity of a narrative, embodied in a single life. The quest for the good life becomes the quest for the best way to live out that unity and bring it to completion.

MacIntyre points out that quests can end in abject failure and frustration, or dissipate into distraction and be abandoned; and human lives may in all these ways also fail. "But the only criteria for success or failure in a human life as a whole are the criteria of success or failure in a narrative or to be narrated quest. A quest for what?"[44]

MacIntyre's answer lies in an examination of the medieval concept of the quest. The first point is that without some concept of a telos, a quest could not begin. A concept of the good for man is needed, and MacIntyre finds this concept in the questioning which led him to search beyond the concept of a practice, for a good to order all goods. The critical point from the medieval concept of the quest is that the goal is not fully characterized, the quest itself yields the understanding of the goal.

> A quest is always an education both to the character of that which is sought and in self knowledge . . . the good life for man is the life spent seeking the good life for man; and the virtues necessary for the seeking are those which will enable us to understand what more and what less the good life for man is.[45]

This represents MacIntyre's concept of the narrative unity of a single life, the telos of which is to search for the good life for man, which is itself the good life for man. Important issues can be raised against this concept. First, MacIntyre concedes that Aristotle's moral scheme rests on three aspects; man-as-he-is, man-as-he-could-be if he realized his telos, and the moral precepts that enable him to pass from the former to the latter. But MacIntyre rejects Aristotle's concept of telos, his metaphysical biology, and without that Aristotle's work becomes unintelligible.[46]

MacIntyre attempts to give an account of the virtues that, "... does not require any identification of any teliology in nature, and hence does not require any allegiance to Aristotle's metaphysical biology."[47] If this attempt fails, the whole scheme of the virtues fail and, in MacIntyre's words, Nietzsche wins.

Bernstein suggests that MacIntyre's telos is very quixotic. It is not based on a Platonic good, that every soul dimly apprehends, or on an Aristotelian good, grasped when we understand the nature of what it means to be a human being. MacIntyre has not shown that there is an objective moral order so, unlike Sophocles, he cannot claim a strong tragic view based on incompatible moral claims made upon us. MacIntyre also fails to address the medieval claim that the good for man is supernatural. Then in a coup de grace Bernstein concludes:

> "When we decipher MacIntyre's provisional conclusion about the good life for man it looks like, despite his intentions, he is making the case for the type of 'decisionism' that he finds so objectionable in Nietzsche and Weber."[48]

The Concept of a Tradition

MacIntyre's third movement in producing a basis for something like Aristotle's concept of the virtues is the concept of a tradition. The tradition serves to link the individual to the larger scheme of community. Good and virtue are not to be exercised just as and for the individual. Each person is a part of the narrative unfolding in the unity of the individual life, and also the presence of a past; a tradition. Everyone is some mother's son, has a country, a past that constitutes the given in a life, the moral starting point.

MacIntyre claims that all kinds of reasoning take place within the context of some traditional mode of thought, transcending through criticism and creativity the limitations of the tradition. A tradition is in good order when it is partly defined by argument within it as to its very meaning and worth. MacIntyre's view contrasts with the Burkeian view of tradition, which opposes reason and conflict with tradition. MacIntyre would clearly define the Burkeian notion of tradition as a dead or dying tradition. A living tradition then is an historically extended, socially embodied argument, partly about the good of that very tradition. An adequate sense of tradition makes the individual aware of the future that the past has made available to the present.[49]

The tradition then is not merely the dead weight of the past. It is a dialogue around a core that even questions its own value. While we live within traditions, roles, and social identities that characterize what we are, they do not determine what we must become. They set the starting point and context for our quest, they do not define it, nor do they define our telos, or what is the good life for us.

The concept of a sport's tradition is well established in contemporary society: the first pitch of the baseball season on opening day, spring football, the Rose Bowl, etc. The tradition helps to order the practice and make the internal good accessible. Violations of tradition usually occur when institutions are in search of more external goods. For example, witness the effects of the demands of television on sporting events. Think of the half-time shows at bowl games, TV time outs, the excesses of the closing ceremonies of the 1984 Los Angeles Olympics. The integrity of the tradition of the practice is sacrificed to increased monetary intake.

MacIntyre's three part framework of something like Aristotle's concept of the virtues is dependent on the virtues themselves. The virtues not only protect the internal good of practices from the corruption of institutions, but also enable the individual to seek his or her own good. More than this, the virtues also sustain the traditions which give the practices and individual lives their necessary historical context.

It is not clear that in his desire to be open ended, MacIntyre has sufficiently delineated what does and does not count as a possible telos of a human life. In fact, Nietzsche would be quite content to work within MacIntyre's scheme.[50]

To Reject Aristotle and Retain MacIntyre's Social Framework

Bernstein has some insightful criticisms of MacIntyre's work. The most significant of which is his failure to escape from Nietzsche. This is due to MacIntyre's understanding of just how central Aristotle's metaphysical biology really is to his morality. Without offering a rational vindication of Aristotle's cosmic order and claims about the truth of human nature, MacIntyre cannot make a rational case for the Aristotelian tradition.[51]

More importantly, Bernstein posits MacIntyre in a tradition, albeit a modern one, of the rage against the Enlightenment or modernity. MacIntyre is sensitive to the fact that every moral philosophy has some particular sociology as its counter part. So he must be aware that the Enlightenment was a legitimate protest against hypocrisy and injustice. One of the main achievements of the Enlightenment was its rebellion against the failures of political and moral ideologies that systematically excluded huge sections of the population from the quest for the good life and made legitimate various forms of inequality and restrictive practices.[52]

MacIntyre himself is writing out of the tradition of the Enlightenment. His concepts of practice, virtue, narrative unity, and tradition admit everyone and deny no one. MacIntyre is aware that previous traditions of the virtues have been based on exclusion.[53]

There is no historical sense in MacIntyre's suggestion that the Enlightenment project was not only mistaken, but that it should never have been commenced in the first place. As Bernstein observes, "To make such a claim, to oppose simply the failures of the 'moderns' with the wisdom of the 'ancients', is to violate MacIntyre's own insistence that we cannot escape our historically." Part of our historicity is the tradition of the Enlightenment, a tradition MacIntyre draws heavily on in his analysis of the virtues.[54]

As we have already noted, MacIntyre acknowledges that Aristotle's ahistorical orientation must be overcome. But the ahistorical nature of Aristotle's work is a central element and without it his work makes no sense. For example, in Aristotle's concept of the virtues, justice was the central virtue. Justice as what each individual deserves, rather than in the universalized form that we now try to implement in our legal system. One of the outstanding features of Aristotle's account of the virtues is the lack of emphasis on rules. Today we often reduce morality to the tendency to obey the law. In the ancient organic society in which Aristotle's virtues were rooted, the very nature of the society provided a rigid framework that contemporary society tries to replace with a legal system. The internalization of the framework of society made the imposition of an outside order redundant to the ancients. Hence, the importance of the virtue of Phroneses, knowing what is due to ones self and others, in the schemes of Aristotle and MacIntyre.

Without an organic society, can Aristotle's concept be strong enough? The root of Aristotle's organic society was his metaphysical biology. Can Aristotle's concept of the virtues still work when the same is due to all people? Perhaps not. Some would say definitely not. If we cannot base what is due to the individual upon the society from which the virtues were projected, can we work our way back into a society through the virtue of conversation, of dialogue? If MacIntyre cannot create the necessary support for his project from a base of something like Aristotle's concept of the virtues, is there an alternative?

Summary

In this chapter, my interpretation of Nietzsche's work has been given; an interpretation of Nietzsche's perspective from my own perspective. An interpretation of Nietzsche is important to this study in its own right, as a powerful indictment of contemporary societal values, but also because the rejection of Nietzsche's perspective is central to MacIntyre's thesis in *After Virtue*. MacIntyre provides a clear explanation of the relationships between practices, institutions, internal and external goods. His model helps to explain how results are valued over performance. However, MacIntyre sees the Nietzschean view of the world as a horrendous and inescapable consequence of the rejection of something like Aristotle's concept of the virtues.

It is my contention that MacIntyre's case for Aristotle is not strong enough and that Nietzsche's work provides the opportunity for the preservation of practices in the jaws of institutions.

CHAPTER 5

Post-Modernity: The Way Forward

As MacIntyre is unable to build a convincing case for something like Aristotle's concept of the virtues, and fails to show that the Enlightenment thinkers were mistaken in rejecting Aristotle in the first place, where do we stand? MacIntyre claims that it was either Aristotle or Nietzsche, with no alternative, and further feels that the horrors of a Nietzschean world of radical individualism are the only possibility without the values of the old world. But MacIntyre failed to appreciate just how dependent upon the concept of the city state, with its metaphysical biology, Aristotle's account of the virtues really is. MacIntyre's modified Aristotle makes no sense in its mutilated state divorced from its own environment.

A third alternative does exist in the form of post-modern philosophy.[1] Working within the Nietzschean world view, post-modern philosophy seeks a new beginning rather than trying to slip an old grounding past the Enlightenment sentries. Post-modern philosophers are not trying to escape the Enlightenment, but save it. They are not rejecting the Nietzschean world but showing its possibilities, showing that it is not necessarily horrendous. On one extreme the attempt is to find a new grounding for values, and on the other extreme to go without a grounding at all. Both rely on authentic communication and values that are created rather than found. In contemporary philosophy these two positions are exemplified in the work of Jurgen Habermas and Richard Rorty.

The importance of post-modern philosophy to this study is simply that it represents the attempt of contemporary thinkers to support values other than the objective, reductionist, and formalistic views that predominate the contemporary North Atlantic culture. These are the same views that have led to the acceptance of winning as excellence and the valuing of results over performance. Habermas and Rorty both present epistemological and ontological escapes and alternatives to these conditions. It is my contention that Habermas' "communicative action" and Rorty's "conversation of philosophy" are closely related to Drew Hyland's "stance of responsive openness". The works of these three men provide a philosophical basis for an alternative to Aristotle in MacIntyre's scheme of practice, tradition, and narrative unity.

Habermas and Rorty attempt to show that the objectivism and formalism of science are only one way of understanding the world, and in doing so they provide an alternative to the valuing of results (objective, external) over performance (subjective, experiential). They show that the view which values results over performance is one view, not athletics' own view. In the terms of Nietzschean perspectivism it is one view amongst many possible views. Habermas and Rorty offer alternative views.

Habermas and Rorty

Habermas, who Richard Bernstein refers to as "the last great rationalist,"[2] is trying to ground post-Enlightenment life in a new critical theory of society. Habermas' critical theory is based on a comprehensive account of rationality with the concept of "communicative action" as its cornerstone. Essentially Habermas is building a rational basis for morality on authentic, uncorrupted, and undistorted communication.

It was one of Habermas' great achievements to link contemporary relevance to the greatest theme of western philosophy. This theme is exemplified by Socrates, who embodied the belief that self-reflection in dialogue can lead to a self-knowledge that will set us free from false opinions and dogma; the belief that we can escape from *doxa* to *episteme*. Thus, undistorted communication becomes even more central and important. Communicative action is such a distinctive type of social interaction that is oriented towards mutual understanding, and distinct from other forms of social interaction oriented towards success, or the achievement of some external goal.

Rorty, on the other hand, wants to deconstruct Philosophy, with a capital "P", and replace it with philosophy. He is not interested in a critical theory of society and opposes system building of all Philosophical kinds. Against Rorty, Habermas looks more like a modern than a post-modern. However, in our narrative, Habermas is a post-modern simply because he does not just accept our Enlightenment heritage, modern society, and modern culture, but wants to go beyond it to construct a new radical basis for community.

Rorty is a philosopher in that he seeks, as Sellars puts it, "to find how things, in the broadest sense of the word, hang together, in the broadest sense of the word."[3] Rorty opposes his position to that of the Philosopher who seeks the Truth about Reality, the True Nature of things. Rorty points out that words like "truth", "good", and "beauty" refer to properties of statements, actions, and things, the commonality of which cannot be identified.[4] There is no common nature of all things that are good, true or beautiful. The quest for such a nature, the search for the Good, the True or the Beautiful as independently existing forms, Rorty identifies as corresponding to the literary genre called Philosophy, which dates roughly from the work of Plato. He does not offer his own theories of Truth, Beauty, and Good, but, rather he thinks that we no longer need to ask questions about them anymore. It will not help us to speak the truth if we study the nature of Truth, nor to act correctly if we study the nature of the Good, nor to appreciate beauty if we study the nature of the Beautiful.

Habermas and Rorty share the view that no one type of knowledge is any more than that—one type of knowledge. Although science has been undeniably successful in predicting and controlling certain aspects of existence, it is not the model for all forms of knowledge. Science is not nature's own language. With the acceptance of scientific knowledge as the model for all legitimate knowledge, there is a corresponding rejection of other validity claims as pseudo- knowledge. For example, in the practical field of historical hermeneutical disciplines the interest is in furthering understanding. Here meaning is not constituted from technical analysis, rather it is concerned with understanding meaning in a particular context. "The verification of lawlike hypotheses in the empirical analytical sciences has its counterpart in the interpretation of texts."[5]

Habermas gives a unity to philosophy, psychology, political science, sociology, and history. This unity is rooted in a vision of mankind drawn from the tradition of German thought that runs from Kant to Marx, a vision that draws its power more from its social and political intention than from the form and system used to present it. The context is more important than the method. In this way Habermas' work can be seen as something other than just another failed attempt of transcending dialectics to ground an alternative scientific method and produce real humanizing knowledge. If we look instead at what he is actually doing, we see interpretative dialectics in action. His early work, with its heavy transcendental undertones, and the more recent scientific orientation of the theory of communicative action, can be seen as stages in the systematic articulation of Habermas' vision of mankind. If there is no transcendental that will allow us God's view of creation then all our knowledge will be subject to update and revision in the same way.[6]

My pragmatic reading of Habermas would be supported by Rorty, as it is this type of self-reflective conversation in the western intellectual tradition that offers us a light in our dark future. But as soon as we try, as the transcendental Habermas does, to ground our conversation we are guilty of the old positivistic hope that we can develop determinate rules that will tell us what is legitimate or authentic communication.

Rorty states that his Pragmatism;

> . . . does not erect science as an idol to fill the place once held by God. It views science as one genre of literature—or to put it in the other way round, literature and the arts as inquiries, on the same footing as scientific inquiries. Thus it sees ethics as neither more "relative" or "subjective" than scientific theory, nor as needing to be more "scientific." Physics is a way of trying to cope with various bits of the universe; ethics is a matter of trying to cope with other bits. Mathematics helps physics do its job; literature and the arts help ethics do its job. Some of these inquiries end up with propositions, some with narratives, some with paintings. The question of what propositions to assert, which pictures to look at, what narratives to tell and comment on and retell, are all questions about what will help us get what we want, or about what we should want.[7]

This is the deconstruction of the western intellectual tradition that Rorty wants to achieve. The point where we see language and all types of vocabulary, physics, art, music, painting, and philosophy as tools to cope with the world, rather than true representation of it, or pieces of truth.

Once we have lost the meta-physical comfort of correspondence theory, must we be left in the Nietzschean world of apocalyptic atheism? Rorty says, "No." Once we see our society, or culture, as something made rather than found, something that is ours, a unique stopping off point, a temporal construction of humanity, then we will regain a commitment to our community and to each other. We will renew, in Rorty's words, "our commitment to other human beings huddled together against the dark."[8]

The whole enterprise of deconstruction is founded on the contingency of our starting place; that we are the living embodiment of the history and beliefs of the culture we are working out of. Our dialogue with other human beings, past and present, is all that we have. To deny this, and seek natural atemporal starting points from another world, is to seek to be a, "properly programed machine", with Philosophy enabling you to, "read your own program."[9]

Thus, a post-Philosophical society, free of the itch for ultimate knowledge, will converse with its past and with itself in a Socratic manner. That is not seeking agreement, but seeking authentic interaction, the virtue of real dialogue rather than the rhetoric of lawyerly debate. The opponents of Rorty's pragmatism will object that this position shows no respect for hard facts, and is not guided from without. To these detractors, Rorty is decadent because he refuses to submit to something "out there."

This is the hard realization that we have nothing at base that we did not put there ourselves, no standard that we did not set, that unites Nietzsche and Rorty. To look out for eternal, natural standards is to be a lover of self-deceptive rhetoric, but to converse with our community to set standards is not to sin against Socrates, but to be truly human and united.

The idea that judgments should not be made in all areas of existence by appeal to objective and external standards gives support to the belief that the scoreboard might not be the best assessment of athletic achievement, and certainly not the only one. The notion of authentic communication and the openness of the conversation of philosophy illustrate the basis from which values can be worked out, created, rather than discovered already existing.

MacIntyre Minus Aristotle, Nietzsche with Community: The Return to the Old Versus the Creation of the New

After reviewing MacIntyre's work and the positions of Habermas and Rorty, all of whom are writing against the Nietzschean background of contemporary society, it becomes apparent that they share some important views. These areas of agreement are best examined through the framework of MacIntyre's *After Virtue* since he has the clearest and most developed position, also because I wish to reject Aristotle and keep Nietzsche and something like the concepts of MacIntyre's framework.

Initially, I wish to address the concept of a tradition. This is evident in the work of all three contemporary philosophers. MacIntyre calls it by name and addresses its significance directly, while Rorty talks more obliquely of the "contingency of starting points." His primary concern with the use of this phrase is to escape the notion of trying to achieve a predetermined perfect state, that we are working out of a specific origin creating our values as conditions evolve rather than trying to be equal to external and eternal dictates. The importance of the tradition is implicit in this stance, the tradition is part of our starting point. Habermas is a fine example of the contingency of starting points, the power of tradition, as he is guided by his own tradition coming out of German thinkers from Kant to Marx. Habermas is guided by this tradition but at the same time he is interacting with it, shaping, and changing it.

MacIntyre claims that a living tradition is evolving, and is at least partly defined by the argument over its own meaning and value. Conversation of an open, Socratic, communicative kind is essential to the health of the tradition. This willingness to talk and weigh the alternatives and their consequences is at the heart of Rorty's and Habermas' work and clearly crucial to MacIntyre's as well. The difference is that MacIntyre seeks to ground this conversation in something like Aristotle's concept of the virtues.

The second important point in MacIntyre's framework is that of the narrative unity of a single human life. As all three men are working out of the tradition of the Enlightenment, they seek to preserve the freedom of the individual while trying to give some meaning to our existence. The concept of the narrative unity would clearly be acceptable to Habermas and Rorty. Habermas feels the greatest attachment to his fellow man, and would probably be content to accept the narrative unity of the individual life as an expression of the individual working his way through the post-modern world. The unity comes from the understanding that the narrative each of us lives, or plays out, is the quest for the good life, and for Habermas this means true communication with our fellows while increasing the application of reasonable behavior.

To Rorty, our narrative is the conversation of the western intellectual tradition, keeping the questions open and the conversation going, exploring all interpretations and positions. The unity comes from our common finitude, and the degree to which we realize our common humanity.

The third, and most basic, unit MacIntyre identifies is the practice. The practice is unalienated *praxis*, a concept Habermas would delight in and Rorty fully understand. Practices turn into meaningless activity when corrupted by institutions. Rorty tells us that this is what happens when the bad guys get the power and we refuse to face up to them. The corruption of practices occurs when the language of science drowns out that of art or hermeneutics.[10]

The practice orders and directs individual and social activity, but it is the sense of a narrative unity, of conversation and relation, that links the practice to tradition. This occurs through the sense of narrative unity that the individual feels. That is why one becomes a practitioner; because the relationship of the individual to the practice can be felt.

The key point of agreement between the three contemporary philosophers is that we must acknowledge the contingency of our starting points, or traditions, of our temporal nature. MacIntyre agrees with Habermas that we cannot judge an act without knowing the agent's intentions and values, which are themselves contingent on traditions. All three contemporary philosophers support the democratization of life and as such are all part of the Enlightenment tradition. MacIntyre's concept of the narrative unity of a single life is mirrored in Rorty's work by his belief that all of our achievements are part of the unfolding of our lives, and purely temporal. To Rorty the purpose of our conversation is to keep the conversation going. It is something worthwhile in itself, a practice through which we can gain internal goods. To Habermas the goal of rational thought is to expand its realm through communicative action. For Habermas and Rorty this is a kind of telos, but for MacIntyre this is not enough. MacIntyre wants an underwriter: Aristotle.

Rorty, more than Habermas or MacIntyre, feels that good is not fated to triumph, and the conversation of the western intellectual tradition might fade away completely. Even MacIntyre concedes that the narrative quest of the individual can, like all quests, fall. This ever present possibility of abject failure is what drove Habermas to look for transcendental guarantees, and MacIntyre to force Aristotle into the twentieth century. They are smuggling metaphysical comfort to a beleaguered post-modern world.

Taking Rorty's hard line that there is nothing out there to which we must be equal, how can we maintain standards, make judgments, and keep the conversation going? The pragmatic Habermas gives us an indication of what is needed and of how hard it is to achieve. MacIntyre looks at social structures that would help. The practice, with its internal good, speaks of the distinction between *techne* and praxis, and MacIntyre wants an Aristotelian set of virtues to link the universal to the particular.[11] The virtues for Aristotle are the means by which a technician becomes a craftsman, and the traditions of the craft continue to evolve as the individual lives out the unity of his life.

Thus, the virtues protect practices from corruption by the institution, and stop the tradition from becoming the dictatorship of the past. But MacIntyre does not provide a strong enough case for Aristotle.

Rorty provides an alternative to Aristotle in the virtue of Socratic dialogue, by which we explore and work out our plans of action. The task of the philosopher becomes that of keeping open the cultural space left by the demise of epistemology, and resist the forces that limit the conversation.[12] We must resist the temptation to substitute "theoria for phronesis."[13]

The virtue of Socratic dialogue is just that, a moral virtue that enables us to carry out our projects, and not something metaphysically or epistemologically grounded.[14] There is no goal as this type of conversation is valid in itself: It is a practice. But more than another practice, it is the practice that can replace the concept of something like Aristotle's view of the virtues in MacIntyre's scheme. The antithesis of Socratic dialogue, or communicative action, is the sullen withdrawal from conversation and community; the closedness to possibilities. The grounds of Socratic dialogue are explored in Hyland's characterization of play as a stance of responsive openness. This forms a basis for gaining internal goods of practices, keeping traditions alive, and communicating authentically. The stance of responsive openness distinguishes the practitioner from the exploiter, and the will to power of the overman enables him to define himself as a practitioner, and resist the corrupting influence of the institution. "For that would be the final abjuration of the notion that truth, and not just power and pain, is to be found out there."[15]

Rorty sees our telos (if he sees us with a telos at all) in the conversation of the western intellectual tradition; MacIntyre sees it in the quest for the good life; Habermas sees it in communicative action; and Hyland sees it in the stance of responsive openness. They are all addressing the same issue from different directions, but their concepts seem applicable and appropriate to each other. We must literally "play" our part in the conversation of our tradition, otherwise the goods internal to the practice will be lost, and undistorted communication will be blocked.

This point is illustrated in the *Razor's Edge* when the Indian riverboatman says to the hero that it must be nice to be rich. Larry replies that he is not rich, and in fact he worked in a coal mine to make the money to pay for his trip to India. "What was the intention?" asks the Indian. Larry replies that he has told him what the intention was, to make money to take the trip. "That was the reason," counters the

Indian. "What was the intention? Without intention work becomes empty motion."[16]

External goods can provide a reason, but internal goods draw intention. Without intention, the understanding of internal goods, our athletic enterprises become empty motion. Without the willingness to converse, our lives become meaningless activity, the dead grist of the positivist's mill. Our lives, our jobs, and our games all become meaningless without the openness to conversation and possibility. The intention is to continue the conversation.

Summary

The practice demands a certain stance of the practitioner. MacIntyre dresses this need in the emotivist terms of moral demands, integrity, honesty, and justice, but it seems perfectly reasonable to suggest that the practice can be maintained from a stance of responsive openness, an authentic play stance. The narrative unity of the individual life and the dialogue of the tradition seem to be areas for the conversation of philosophy, or communicative action. If a modified Aristotle fails, what then are the chances for a modified Nietzschean view? A post-modern conception of the telos for man, where the conversation of the narrative and the tradition need not be grounded, but just need to continue authentically and without metaphysical comfort. If Aristotle cannot be persuaded to join us in the contemporary world, can Nietzsche's contemporaries help us find *a good* for man, rather than *the good* for all men? The internal good available to the athlete through his practice would then be related to the authenticity of the dialogue of the athlete with the craft.

CHAPTER 6

Sport as a Form of Contemporary Community

We will now explore the possibilities offered to sport in the philosophical stances that have been examined. I will suggest that the Nietzschean view of art as the true medium for understanding human existence calls for the athlete to be viewed as a performing artist, and, as such, can link a Nietzschean individual into MacIntyre's framework of practice, narrative unity, and tradition without recourse to Aristotle. This conception is supported philosophically and Philosophically by a Rortyian pragmatic style.

Nietzsche told us long ago that the values of the past are dead, and looked to man to create his own values. MacIntyre sought to ground our choices in something external, but ended up with too much subjectivity for his own taste. Rorty seeks to free us from external grounding, all grounding, and to create conditions for the conversation of the western intellectual tradition to continue. The problem being dealt with in all of this is poetically and simply expressed by Gary Smith. "If there is justice in the sky a man can accept limits on his freedom. If there is not . . . "[1]

This is the root of the Nietzschean world, both of vulgar and tender Nietzscheanism. It is the fearful emptiness of the possibility of unrestrained self-interest, and the possibility of true human freedom. The implications for sport are important and interesting. The vulgar Nietzschean world points to the horror of the overman as athlete; the use of raw power to subjugate the opponent and increase personal power. The tender Nietzschean world frees the overman as creative athlete, making his own values and transcending the arbitrary limitations of society.

The Horror of the Overman as Athlete

This concept is rooted in the vulgar Nietzschean reading of what must be the consequences of Nietzsche's world. The radical individualism that MacIntyre hates so much is taken to lead to single minded pursuit of self-interest. A world without values "in the sky" is taken as a world without values. A world where the powerful emotivist's techniques will convince others of the morality and fairness of his own actions. From such a position are born the contemporary "philosophical" maxims of, "looking out for number one," and "do unto others before they do unto you." This is a world that Sadler describes as embodying a Having cultural type, where what you own or consume defines your worth, and where there is no importance attached to how the power to own or consume is achieved. Science is valued for its power to produce and control rather than for its descriptive role.

Against such a background Keating's model of athletic excellence as winning is quite at home, but his philosophical support of this type of cultural value is just a symptom of how pervasive the rhetoric of competition and victory has become. Not only is winning taken to be the very core of athletic excellence, but this value is extended into all relationships in the rational pursuit of any interest. The radical individualist, freed from constraints, acts in selfish self-interest. This vulgar Nietzschean world has a climate of unrestrained physical, social, and economic violence where the powerful destroy the weak just because they can; where the strong necessarily subjugate the powerless.

The overman as an athlete in this world is an animal who seeks to punish opponents. He takes the opportunity to inflict pain and revels in 'beating' friends and foes alike. Intimidation is the watchword of this environment. Never mind 'psyching out' an opponent so his distracted state or nervousness interfere with his performance. In this realm the overman terrifies his opponents. A large crowd of spectators makes one nervous, but terror at the prospect of being injured and tortured by an animal that feels no humane restraints on its behavior is something else. "But that is not part of the game!" you protest. Game? Games are social events, these men are warriors intent on prospering at the expense of others. Victory in the contest is excellence, and excellence through the exercise of animal power can open many doors to power in society as a whole.

Loyalty to these vulgar Nietzscheans is not to the spirit of the game. For them the game is just a point in society where their particular style of violence is made legitimate. Loyalty is not to the team owner, as he is just another type of animal who savages with his checkbook power instead of physical power. Loyalty is not to the team, as they are united for the length of the game by a common intent, but they are competitors for places on the team, and teams trade players so often that one day's team mate is the next day's opponent. Loyalty is only to the self. But how could one be loyal to one's self and continually put it in such danger? Loyalty is to the exercise of power, it is the duty of the overman to crush that which is weaker: "That which does not kill me makes me stronger."[2] Power and victory on the field lead to power and wealth off the field. Money is power throughout society and the game is a way to power. There is no concept here of internal goods from the practice, and if you find an opponent who thinks such things exist then so much the better for you; he is a sap, a fool, a wimp. There is one born every minute to fall to the animal's claws.

The power of money is omniscient, it dictates to the game. Television money changes times and dates of games, alters the form of events, commodifies the whole experience, commodifies the athlete, markets him, and describes him in terms that are not his own. Yet he cannot see the damage that is done in this process for he is compensated. Marx's critique of capitalist exploitation and alienation of the worker by the owner deals with this situation as it happened to evolve in the west. However, control of production by the workers, where it has been tried, has not proven sufficient to free the worker. The animal cannot be freed, *he is free*.

When realization hits the athlete-warrior-animal we see characters like Maxwell in *North Dallas Forty* who concludes a soul searching discussion with Elliot on the phoney, exploitative, and dehumanizing nature of pro football by chiming, "Hell! We're all whores, we might as well be the best!"[3] A more devastating example is found in Marlon Brando's character in *Apocalypse Now*. He is the quintessential killing machine, his powers and experiences have taken him beyond good and evil, and he knows that the morality that guides nations and individuals is mythic and a hypocrisy. This realization is a terrifying abyss that threatens to swallow all. To the army, with its herd morality, he is no hero, but a murderer. But he understands them, while they cannot understand him![4]

The Creative Possibilities of the Overman as Athlete

What then could be the creative possibilities of the overman as athlete when the horrors seem inescapable? Make no mistake, the horror is real, and always possible, but not necessary in any logical sense. The creativity of the overman as superior athlete is rooted in the "will to power" as power over the self and not as power over others. The "will to power" here refers to the creativity to define yourself in your own terms and not to let others define you for yourself. This is manifested in an internal drive and control that sets higher standards, levels of dedication, achievement, and discipline for the self rather than for others. This "will to power" is a neutral force. It is not in and of itself good or evil, but beyond good and evil. Nietzsche took this force to be the key mover in human existence. But how it is directed is a separate issue. Nietzsche clearly believed that the control and definition of the self was the true use of the "will to power." To control and subjugate others was to abuse it in some way.

The Nietzschean "will to power," the ability of the individual to define his existence in his own terms, is the root of the ability of the practitioner to maintain the practice against the encroachment and corruption of the institution. Thus, the "will to power" is not the ability to dominate others, but to dominate and define oneself, the power to be, to resist corruption: integrity.

From this position it is clear that the tender Nietzschean athlete, the creative overman as athlete, is directed from the desire to conquer his inner world, while the horror of the vulgar Nietzschean athlete stems from his treating of the world as a means to his ends. The creative aspect of the overman will be in harmony with the concept of a practice because he is motivated by intrinsic expression and creativity.

The creative overman is of course living against the same dark, valueless backdrop of existence that the vulgar Nietzschean delights in, where power can always he wielded by animals masquerading as people. The difference is that the tender Nietzschean uses his freedom from arbitrary values imposed from without to create and define himself in his own terms. The radical liberal individualism of postmodern society, with its de facto relativism and emotivism, is seen by the vulgar Nietzscheans as an easy place in which to live, and to make decisions about values. It is easy because there is nothing to guide one's actions save for one's own interests. Nothing to judge those actions by except their efficacy in achieving arbitrarily chosen ends. How then could decisions be difficult? (Except, perhaps, to choose the most efficient means to your ends.) On the other extreme the tender Nietzschean sees it as a hard place to live and make value decisions, precisely because there is nothing to guide save for personal desires and interests. Finding yourself and your way, weighing the consequences of your acts and beliefs, agonizing over the choices before you, is hard but authentic. Your values are presented in your actions, and that is how you will be regarded and understood.

I choose the word 'agonizing' deliberately to describe the choices in the Nietzschean world because there is a hint of that recurring refrain of this narrative in it. "Agony," means severe pain, or a bursting forth of emotion, and derives its origin from the Greek "Agon," a contest. We literally face a contest between possible courses of action, and the result of making a considered opinion in which one weighs the consequences is an emotionally rendering experience. The easy decision is made when one is already closed to the issue and driving for a determined outcome. For instance the bigot would not vote for the Reverend Jesse Jackson in a Presidential primary because he is black. But the decision is complicated for the serious member of the society because, although Jackson may seem the most able candidate for office, the racism of the nation may guarantee a Republican victory if Jackson is the Democratic Presidential candidate. Thus, being open to the possibilities results in an agonizing choice, while being closed makes life easy. The re-occuring refrain that I spoke of is that of the stance of responsive openness. The tender Nietzschean is open to possibilities in the maelstrom of life, while the vulgar Nietzschean is closed to possibilities other than the pursuit of personal selfish interests.

The athlete can transcend the herd morality, and empirical evidence exists to show that top athletes can often violate laws with relative impunity, or at least receive minimal punishment. On a more positive level, the creative overman as athlete can move beyond the confines of societal convention, using his power to act and achieve beyond the tradition. He can transcend barriers of racism and live with less restrictions, a model of freedom to the herd.

For example, NFL football stars are able to achieve great things for humane causes because they can cut through red tape and act. Herschel Walker used his overman creativity to dance with the Dallas Ballet. Paul Brietner, the West German soccer player, retired from soccer after playing in the World Cup winning team of 1974 to work with mentally handicapped children. He returned to the National team in 1982 and played on the team that finished as runners-up. He returned to that arena because his work with the mentally handicapped children needed more financial aid. The warrior took up the sword again but in the name of the innocent.

Another example of this type of transcendental power is manifested in the 1987 European Footballer of the Year, Holland and AC Milan's Ruud Gullit. Upon receiving his award Gullit promptly dedicated it to the imprisoned South African black leader Nelson Mandela. Gullit's father is from Surinam, his mother from Holland, and he sports a mop of dreadlocks to compliment his racial mix. He lives in Milan where he enjoys the sophistication of the city, and he can converse fluently in five languages. This man has transcended the description by which others define him; a black soccer player of enormous talent. He has defined himself as a world citizen larger than the confines of international soccer.[5]

Given this freedom, or realizing this freedom, the athlete can create his own description of himself and transcend the descriptions that others apply to him, and authentically express his being. Thus the "will to power" can be a form for creativity and authenticity, and not necessarily a tool of oppression.

The narrative of the individual describing and creating himself in his own terms is compatible with MacIntyre's concept of the narrative unity of a single human life within an evolving tradition. This self-creation is a value inherent in all practices, and is a type of internal good. But there is no guarantee of success in the pursuit of this good; there is no success except perhaps the attempt to achieve it. This effort accepts that there is no truth out there, or within us, waiting to be discovered. There is only what we create, and that means that "out there" is only power and pain.[6] Oppression and liberation are only names of aspects of power that we do and do not like.[7]

One of the consequences of failing to understand this last point can be seen in the opposition to the alternative, Bohemian, lifestyle of the counter culture developed by the overman as athlete. What Jurgen Habermas calls the neo-conservative backlash. This is a reaction born out of the acceptance of modern society, but a rejection of modern culture. The neo-conservative is a liberal who lost his nerve when faced with the cultural consequences of modernity, and who tries to return to the traditional values of the past.[8]

The functions Habermas ascribes to the avant garde artist, giving ". . . authentic expression to experiences which he makes via a decentered subjectivity freed from the pressures and exigencies of everyday knowledge and practice,"[9] could be applied to the creative overman and athlete. Freed by his "will to power" and transcending cultural barriers and values, the overman stands in the possibility of this relationship with society.

However, the neo-conservative treats the symptoms and not the cause when he attacks the avante garde artist, or athlete, as Habermas points out:

> In the place of the economic and administrative imperatives, the so called objective exigencies, which monetarize and bureaucratize growing dimensions of life and increasingly transform relationships into commodities and objects of administration—in the place of

these real sources of social crisis, they (neo-conservatives) focus on the spectre of an expansive and subversive culture.[10]

This situation is doubly destructive, as not only is the "subversive culture" not the cause of the problems of contemporary society, but it also offers the most fertile ground from which the vocabularies and languages that might help us cope with our lives could emerge. The whole of Critical Theory after Marx was devoted to developing a critique of instrumental rationality, with the idea of laying the groundwork for an alternative and humane society.[11]

The creativity of the overman is no more a necessary development from the nihilist world of Nietzsche than the horror of the overman. One is our greatest hope while the other our constant fear. As Nietzsche says, "What makes one heroic?—Going out to meet at the same time one's greatest sorrow and one's greatest hope."[12] On a collective level we need to create an environment that will encourage one condition and discourage the other, it is this hope that calls so strongly in the work of MacIntyre. On an individual level the stance of responsive openness seems to be a basis for the creative overman, and the closed stance that sullenly refuses to enter a dialogue seems to be the basis of the horrors of the overman. The stance of openness and willingness to hold yourself and your position open to question, is thus opposed by a dogmatic closeness of fixed belief and intractable positions.

Gary Smith's study of heavyweight boxing champ Mike Tyson contains elements of both the creativity and horror of the overman as athlete champion. Tyson is the product of an environment and a culture where power is exercised because it can be exercised. Tyson fights not out of instinct but out of "outraged innocence;" he is justice in the world, he fights for the people from the broken Brownsville tenement landscape.[13]

"This world is evil, this world is sick, they rip heads off birds, they put poison in aspirin, they murder little boys . . . Somebody's got to stop it, nobody will stop it, I will stop it, I will be justice, I will repay them all."[14]

Interestingly, Habermas claims that, "communicative reason acts in history as an avenging force."[15] Gary Smith continues:

> In my mind everyone is against me . . . I love the smell of danger. I love being on the edge . . . I believe in taking chances. There is nothing I won't try as far as my social life. Small stakes don't interest me. Only big. I never stole for money, I stole for excitement. No one

will ever tell me what to do . . . I am the bad guy, I want to be the bad guy . . . *but I'm not the bad guy.*[16]

He laughs and grabs his listeners shoulder, his head nuzzles against it, almost like a puppy. Does anyone understand how painful it is to be *this*,—and in the blink of an eye or the ring of a bell to be its inverse.[17]

These paragraphs artistically express the conflict within a single man between the characteristics of the creative and vulgar overman. Tyson is torn by the joy of being that iron-hard, thrill-seeking animal, and the horror of being that same animal. He is torn by the necessity of being extremely violent on cue, and his desire to be soft and loving. A conflict that was tragically illustrated in Tyson's 1992 rape conviction, both in the act of rape and in the extremely polarized responses of the public.

Athlete as Artist

Both Nietzsche and Rorty take the artist rather than the scientist as the hero of mankind. Both support the vision of the artist as a more valid medium for understanding ourselves, a creative and expressive view rather than a reductionist one. The possibility of taking the artist as a model of the athlete is clearly indicated by the previous examination of the creative overman as athlete. The overman as athlete is creative in the positive sense of creating himself, but can he also be creative in the expressive, interpretive, and communicative sense we usually conceive of the artist?

Much has been written about the relationship of sport to art, usually in the form of citing examples of similarities between the two. On the one hand, the artistic elements of sport are pointed out, and, on the other, the sportive elements of art are identified. If sufficient similarities exist, it will be claimed that sport and art are related in some essential way.[18]

But what is to count as art in the first place is problematic. This is due, in part, to the refusal of the artists to accept limits or parameters on their endeavors. Arbitrary limits are rejected, and "rules of art" are continually violated. This dynamic aspect of the tradition of art is the root of the practice's avante garde and Bohemian counter culture that the neo-conservatives find so threatening. It is this very nature of art as an ongoing conversation that proves it is alive as a tradition. As a basic premise, art requires a human creator, and it is not legitimate to view something as a work of art unless it was intended as such.[19] There is also a need to distinguish between the aesthetic and artistic. David Best states that the aesthetic:

> "Applies to sunsets, birdsong, and mountain ranges, whereas the artistic is limited at least in its sensual uses to artifacts or performances intentionally created by man."

As an extension of this distinction, Best concludes that sport cannot be an art form because it does not . . . "allow for the possibility of the artist's comment through his art on life situations."[20]

However, this view only follows from an idealist conception of art that demands certain forms and contents in a process for it to be called art. Sport is not necessarily art anymore than painting is necessarily art. But if the intention of the creator is to act as an artist, then sport has the potential to serve as his medium. Best's inability to see artistic expressions or comments on life situations in an athletic performance is entirely his own failing due to his setting of arbitrary boundaries in demarking ideal forms.

The question is now raised about how certain "accepted" art forms actually comment on life situations, and abstract works are an obvious example. Deconstructionists would, of course, attack Best's notions that the comment in art is contained within the work, and would maintain that the meaning is found in the individual interacting with the work. There is nothing fixed and held in the art work for us to decode, there is only our interaction with the piece.

Best claims that there is an aesthetic aspect to sport but not an artistic aspect. He then contrasts aesthetic sport with purposive sport:

> Briefly in purposive sport there is a means/ends distinction. For instance, the end which at least largely defines the character of soccer, namely scoring goals, can be achieved by various means. It makes perfect sense for the soccer manager to tell his team that he doesn't care how they score, how ugly and clumsy are their methods, as long as they do score more goals than their opponents. By contrast, it would make no sense to say to an artist that it does not matter how she achieves the purpose of her work. And similarly it would make no sense to say to a gymnast or diver that it does not matter how he or she achieves the purpose of the activity, since achievement in such aesthetic sports is inseparably bound up with the manner in which one performs.[21]

Best's view of soccer is answered by Rorty when he says that the anti-pragmatist (I think Best fits this bill) is like ". . . the basketball player who thinks that the reason for playing the game is to make baskets. He mistakes an essential moment in the course of an activity for the end of the activity."[22]

Best is clearly in the Keating "winning is excellence", camp. A further example of a Having type cultural value; it does not matter how you have what you have, just that you have it. While Best is correct as far as pointing out that there are no points for style in soccer and other so called "purposive sports," the manner in which one goes about the task is just as important in purposive as "aesthetic sports." Furthermore, there is an undeniable aesthetic element in soccer, while it is not required intrinsically in the game, nor rewarded extrinsically. From MacIntyre's perspective the pursuit of this aesthetic aspect of sport is partly what maintains it as a practice, and keeps it from becoming meaningless except as a vehicle for obtaining external goods.

Athletes have the right to be viewed as artists if they so wish, if that is how they define themselves. But whether or not their art is of high quality is as contingent as any other artist's work. For the ancient Greeks, the artist was an artisan, and occupied an inferior position in Greek society relative to contemporary western society. The enjoyment of art ". . . did not stand upon the same level as enjoyment (and engagement) in rational thought and contemplative insight."[23]

This position is rooted in Socrates' epic battle with the poets. Socrates took the work of artists to be imperfect representations of illusions. That is to say the physical world is an imperfect reflection of the ideal word, and the artists give their own imperfect expressions of the imperfect world. Socrates thought that the way to know truth and reality was through rational thought, so the mind was taken as superior to the physical word, and thus, to the body.

This elevation of reason over art incensed Nietzsche because he took art to be the true vehicle of humanity, and because the Socratic/Platonic/Aristotelian view denied the possibility of tragedy. To these ancient Greeks, tragedy was the conflict of virtues, and this, of course, was impossible in their world views. But to Nietzsche, tragedy is our essence, as there are continual clashes of contradicting demands placed upon us because there is no ordering value, or valuing order.

Against this background of chaos, the Nietzschean overman makes order, albeit of limited scope and range. The artist makes order on the canvas, the poet in the verse, and the athlete on the field. The creative potential of the athlete forging order out of chaos is the potential to be artistic. However, the medium of sport for artistic endeavor neither requires nor necessitates that all athletes be artists. Ballet does not make every dancer a prima ballerina, nor opera every singer a prima donna, nor orchestral work of every violinist a virtuoso. Neither do all athletes play central expressive roles in the play of the game, but they help provide the framework for the artistry of those who do have central expressive roles. The total endeavor is the art, the practice, and it is maintained in part by the efforts of those who will dedicate themselves to supporting roles. The perfect blend for a soccer team has been described as eight road sweepers and three violinists.[24] The art lies in the relationship of the individual and the craft. The game of soccer can highlight human feelings of courage, self-sacrifice, and triumph. Playing style can reflect the values of the players and spectators. Vignettes of incredible vision and ability, timed and delivered with excruciating accuracy, can extend the powers of the artist over space and time on the field.

The people who sympathize with Best's view probably would also object to other contemporary cultural manifestations such as rock music, as well as sport and art. Their feelings are expressed by Allan Bloom who says of rock music and videos that there are, ". . . three great lyrical themes: sex, hate, and a smarmy, hypocritical version of brotherly love. Such polluted sources issue in a muddy stream where only monsters can swim." Bloom follows this statement with a startling, and horrifying, confirmation of his elitist view of art when he claims "Nothing noble, sublime, profound, delicate, tasteful or even decent can find a place in such tableaux. There is room only for the intense, changing, crude, and immediate, which Tocqueville warned us would be the character of democratic art . . ."[25]

Christopher Lasch attacks this elitist view of art that promotes it beyond the everyday into the realm of high culture. He seeks a truly democratized art as an antidote to the conceptions of Best and Bloom. For him the apotheosis of art and the degradation of work went hand in hand. Work has become so mind numbing, Lasch suggests, that art has been promoted as the means to ameliorate the working existence. However, art is produced by experts, in an extension of the division of labor, and it is stored in special buildings where we may visit it to pay homage. The artist is promoted to an elite position, a far cry from his status in ancient Greece. Objects of art then become commodities for the conspicuous consumption of the wealthy who are thus able to make a statement about their own importance.

> The democratization of leisure has not democratized the consumption of high culture, and, even if it had, the creation of a broader audience for the arts would not restore the connection between art and everyday life, on which the vitality of art demands. Works of art,

as Dewey put it, "idealize qualities found in common experience."
When they lose touch with common experience, they become her-
metic and self-referential, obsessed with originality at the expense
of communicability . . .[26]

Lasch's aim is to put art back into work, or make work artistic in
a restoration of craftsmanship. If art is to idealize common experiences, then sport serves this function on various levels for much of
society. But how can we characterize the artistic athlete from the non-
artistic athlete? Hyland's concept of play seems to apply here. If an
athlete plays, that is, holds the stance of responsive openness, is he not
also going to be expressive and creative? It seems to be that to hold the
play stance is to be a practitioner, that is, motivated by goods internal
to the task, to be truly a quester for excellence, to be the creative
overman and the artistic athlete. All of these conditions are different
facets of the same type of existence.

Play and art are united in nature but divided in medium. So, in
as much as sport can be a vehicle for play, it is also an art form. Art
without responsive openness is mere production. Is copying a great art
work art itself? The copier is closed to all possibilities except the end
of reproducing a copy of the original. It is a technical exercise. Without
intention, work, art, or sport become meaningless activity. With the
intention to be artistic the athlete can be so considered.

It may be argued that athletes cannot be performing artists, but
that they may well be craftsmen. But to Lasch, Rorty, and Nietzsche,
craftsmen are artists by virtue of their relationship to their chosen
tasks. We can all be artists then, someone might complain. Yes, we
can, with a stance of responsive openness and striving to turn our lives
into works of art. We can fulfill Nietzsche's dream, and live as artistic
Socrates.

Sport as a Practice

In MacIntyre's work the concept of a practice is explained as a
coherent human activity that involves the use of technical skill to
achieve internal standards of excellence. The pursuit of which yields
access to goods internal to the practice that could not be gained in any
other way than participation in the practice. MacIntyre states that the
internal goods are not the exclusive, or even necessary, possessions of
the *best* participants in the activities that constitute a practice. Which
is to say that the most effective and technically adept athletes, the

persistent winners, are not necessarily even true practitioners. They may solely use the practice as a means to external goods, such as power, money, and fame that may be available through the associated institution.

While the institution views the practice as a means to external ends, it should also be remembered that the practice cannot survive for long without an institutional framework. The institution is interested in external goods not internal ones, and as long as the practice/product "sells" the institution will not be concerned by alterations and modifications to the form of the activity. Under this influence the practice is commodified and sold. This was clearly illustrated in the discussion in chapter 2 concerning the effects of capitalism on sport and athletes.

During the last twenty years, even sports that grew out of a counter culture have become institutionalized; such as surfing and frisbee games. Both have international governing boards to control them and an industry built up to supply them.[27]

It is something of a tragic situation then that the true practitioner, dedicated, training, honing his skills, and deepening his understanding of the practice and himself, will always be exploited to some extent by the institution. This may lead to an alienation of the athlete from the sport as he realizes the relationship of institution to practice in his own situation. Peter Gent's novel, *North Dallas Forty*, provides an account of just such a realization, as one player comes to see that the "game" of the NFL is played in the front office by the owners and administrators, while the players are just the equipment to be used and cast aside when worn out or broken. The owner warns the athlete that seeing through the game is not the same as winning the game. A statement that personal growth and understanding is of course secondary to maintaining the illusion that the practice is still intact.[28]

In a sports world dominated by institutions, the only important thing is the maximization of profits, more and more money from the toys of the wealthy, not craftsmanship or the practice; not the internal goods. Practitioners can be corrupted by the power of the institution's views to the point that when players take the field with the sole intention of winning, they will violate the rules, opponents, teammates, themselves, and the practice itself. All are mere obstacles to be overcome in the drive to achieve external goods.

MacIntyre seeks to prevent this by invoking something like Aristotle's concept of the virtues, but he fails to convince us that a mutilated Aristotelianism is something that maintains even its internal consistency. We do need justice, honesty, and courage but these are simply virtues that can no longer be grounded in Greek metaphysics anymore. There virtues are an integral part of keeping the conversation of philosophy going, of communicative action, and authentic communication. The stance of responsive openness is rooted in these virtues, the openness to the consequences of our actions. But they are simply virtues, they are aspects of the use of power that we like; but they do not exist outside of us.

The practice provides a framework for ordering our lives and guiding our actions. A practitioner has a theme to his life and orders his existence to the service of the practice. The choice of a practice will be determined by the particular social and historical situation of each individual, as well as his interests and talents. But what ever the chosen practice, the practitioner will have to submit, at least initially, to the existing standards of excellence and wisdom of the practice.

The question could be raised as to whether or not sport really has internal goods. The answer really depends here on which side of the institution/practice divide you stand. The goods internal to sport are unique to sport, so to say they revolve around satisfaction and craftsmanship is only part of the story. The goods internal to sport lie in the athlete's relationship to his craft and the particular type of satisfaction and interaction that comes from the specific situation of that practice. The goods come from participation in the interaction with the contents of the practice and the other practitioners, and not just from achieving the internal standards of excellence. The quest for those goods yields the other internal goods.

The Narrative Unity of a Single Life

The concept of the narrative unity of a single life is the way in which the individual exists within the demands of the practice. Instead of being a fixed commodity, only of value at certain times, the idea of the narrative acknowledges the temporal and linear nature of our existence. The institution, however, would view an athlete as a nobody who is discovered and shot to stardom, only to be returned to insignificance as his powers decline with age or injury. Practices, by contrast, support the narrative view, that of the child growing and learning, developing interests and abilities; tracing an ancient path through apprenticeship to young man full of power and running, growing to adulthood with increased powers and knowledge, then gradually into old age making that immortal trade of physical power for increased knowledge. But all the time there is an individual traveling this path, not a series of different types of person. The individual lives out a narrative, a quest for excellence and the good life within the framework of the practice, all the time interacting with the tradition and standards of the practice, helping to set them as well as submitting to them. Thus, the athlete as practitioner is not just following a prescribed path but creating his own quest, so that his own story is self-contained, but told against the backdrop of the practice. The athlete describes and, thus, creates himself in his own terms. His narrative is his own, but also part of that of the practice.

The emphasis is clearly on the process of exploring personal potential and the medium of the practice, and not merely the achievement of victory, of games won and money made. The emphasis is on the internal goods of the practice, the possibilities within the game of self-expression, the chance of transcending the limits of the game, and of playing with that effortless effort in the artless art. What we might describe as letting the game play you. This is the highest peak of athletics and not victory in the contest. This is the overman at his most creative, with power over himself to go beyond the good and bad of the practice and play directly with the game.[29]

The Tradition

The tradition that the practice represents is not the dead voice of the past forcing through entrenched power the complicity of the present. It is the possibilities of the future that the past has made available to the present. The practice is a framework in which the unity of the individual narrative plays out. The tradition is the framework in which the practice plays out its own narrative from past to future.

This narrative is guided and defined by argumentation and discussion about the very nature of the tradition and practice itself, and this represents a live tradition. A dead tradition allows no authentic dialogue; a dead tradition is a dictatorship. The live tradition is an ongoing conversation without an end.

The problem MacIntyre faces is that he bases the continuing existence of the tradition and practice on a grounding in Aristotle's virtue. To seek a grounding is to return to the notion that values are found rather than created. Rorty would say that we need to converse authentically and make our values, and not appeal to the authority of something outside of us. But this also means not submitting to the claims and lures of external goods. As Bloom says, "True openness means closeness to all the charms of the present."[30] We cannot ground and guarantee the basis of the tradition and the practice, but we can struggle to bring about what we think are the best alternatives. This is found in a careful choice between alternative possibilities.

The world of the sports practice is an interplay between opponents and a dialogue amongst teammates, each living out a narrative unity within the practice, which is situated in a larger tradition. The tradition is also in a dialogue with itself and its practitioners from a historical and social perspective. The tradition is the possibilities of the future made available to the present by the past.

◆ ◆ ◆

Out on that practice field, in the cool pool of light that splits the darkness, the athletes weave the patterns of the game. In a ritual of action, they unfold their relationship to the practice and each other. The seasons sweep, and the sweet smell of juicy summer grass finds them with shirts off, but wearing a layer of sweat. The fall rains beat on the hoods of the rainsuits and the playing surface is slick, opening once again that chapter of interplay with mud. The winter snows have to be heavy, or the frozen ground rutted, to drive them from that pool of night brightness. But always, the relationship of the player to the craft, and the practitioners are there, rain or shine, to make those magical touches on the ball and drive themselves further and deeper into themselves, the practice, and the tradition.

Conclusion

"Not every end is a goal. The end of a melody is not its
goal: but nonetheless, if the melody had not reached
its end it would not have reached its goal either."

—Nietzsche, *The Wanderer and His Shadow.*

I have suggested that the stance of responsive openness is a
position in which one is open to the participation in internal goods of
a practice. Therein lies the key to understanding where this quality
has been lost in the past. The intentionality of the individual determines the relationship and possibility of internal good, the practice,
and the individual. Power is not good or evil; art is not contained in
techniques; play is not defined by activities; these qualities are
products of the stance, the relationship of the individual to his chosen
task. Suppression and liberation are just aspects of power that we do
or do not like. Art is that which expresses and communicates a view,
values, or feelings from a stance of responsive openness. Art and play
are not necessarily contained in those activities we usually associate
with them, although they may well be the most frequently chosen
vehicles. The stance and intention of the individual is both the thread
that links play, art, and craftsmanship, and the basis of these.

In the post-philosophical, post-modern, deconstructed world, a
craftsman is an artist. The works of the Philosopher are not necessarily more essential to philosophy than the thoughts of ordinary people.
In this world the intention and explorations of the athlete can be as
artistic as those of the great dancer or sculptor. The value of the
enterprise does not lie in conformity to found standards, external and
eternal to our existence. The worth is not in trying to be equal to an
ideal form from the divine banquet. Success does not reside in getting

109

it right, but in exploring the possibilities in dialogue with our fellows. The practice as conceived by MacIntyre shows us a framework for the pursuit of internal goods, the relationship of the doer to the done. The narrative unity and tradition show us the temporal nature of our own existence, but at the same time help us to place ourselves in the narrative sweep of a larger unfolding. The ideas of the conversation of philosophy, authentic dialogue, and communicative action all point to the communication between individuals in stances of responsive openness.

As we live out our lives we live out our own narrative. We become the cutting edge of a tradition as we apply ourselves to our chosen tasks, our practices, and simultaneously continue and change the tradition and the practice. But to preserve the internal goods of the practice we must resist the siren call of external goods alone, and the slick easy answers of the institution. The determination to preserve the practice and the bond between practitioners is the basis of true community. So if the practice fails, and becomes dominated by the institution, then the basis of true community is lost along with the internal goods.

There are no guarantees here, there is no way to underwrite all this so that the good guys win. This was to be Aristotle's role in MacIntyre's scheme. The lack of metaphysical comfort represents our greatest challenge. We must live and act without sinning against our heritage while knowing that our heritage is just one example of humanity, and not the final or "correct" example. Without metaphysical comfort we must order our own world, what we are cowardly enough to allow we will surely get, and that which we are courageous enough to oppose may be overcome. Nietzsche warned us of the failure to assert one's rights;

> To exercise power costs effort and demands courage. That is why so many fail to assert rights to which they are perfectly entitled— because a right is a kind of power but they are too lazy or too cowardly to exercise it. The virtues which cloak these faults are called patience and forebearance.[1]

Furthermore, there is no appeal to the sky for justice. To reach this point in the unfolding of the western intellectual tradition has taken great sacrifice by many, many heroes. If we let the institutions overrun the practices, if we let the characters of the emotivist society project their images of personality on our 26-inch Sony cave wall, then we are failing our heritage. This is what MacIntyre alluded to when he says at the end of *After Virtue:*

> What matters at this stage is the construction of local forms of community within which civility and the intellectual and moral life can be sustained through the new dark ages which are already upon us. And is the tradition of the virtues was able to survive the horrors of the last dark ages, we are not entirely without grounds for hope. This time, however, the barbarians are not waiting beyond the frontiers; they have already been governing us for quite some time. And it is our lack of consciousness of this that constitutes part of our predicament.[2]

All we can ask of each other is to keep the conversation going in the face of the fear and doubt. Is this then a pessimistic view? No, but we must not delude ourselves that it will be easy. But to close ourselves to our possibilities and to refuse to play and create is to betray Socrates and our heritage. Jacob Bronowski, a man who worked heroically to provide a unified view of art and science, concludes his majestic *Ascent of Man* with these words,

> We are all afraid—for our confidence, for the future, for the world. That is the nature of the human imagination. Yet every man, every civilization, has gone forward because of its engagement with what it has set itself to do. Knowledge is not a looseleaf notebook of facts. Above all it is a responsibility for the integrity of what we are, primarily of what we are as ethical creatures. The personal commitment of a man to his skill, the intellectual commitment and the emotional equipment working together as one.[3]

It is no argument to dismiss this whole narrative, and say that results are valued over performance, and winning taken as excellence, because that is the way the world is. That is not the way the world is. That is the way we have made the world.

The existentialist might feel justified in retreating into himself when confronted with the daunting prospect of the task of reshaping the world. But it is a task that starts from an existential position, the stance of responsive openness, and works from there out into relationships and interactions with the world. The institutions will not be overthrown, they will be undermined, they will become vestigial, and no longer needed.

How can people who oppose this view be convinced? This question will be answered with another one. What do we do when the best liberal democratic education leaves the child a violent criminal? We must hold our position open to question, and face the challenge with an acknowledgment that we may be wrong. We cannot invoke transcendental law to support our position, but we can offer pragmatic argument that might convince by its overall plausibility. Alexander Nehamus identifies that stance in the work of Nietzsche, and calls it perspectivism.[4] There is no guarantee of success, all that we can do is maintain the integrity of what we do, maintain the practices. There are no quick and easy answers, and it was the desire for these, and the illusion that they could be found, that created our contemporary turmoil. The answers will come, if at all, as Rorty says, "only by a slow and painful choice between alternative self-images."[5]

Notes

Introduction

1. Phil Soar, Martin Tyler, and Richard Widdows, *The Hamlyn World Encyclopedia of Football* (London: Hamlyn, 1984), 105.

2. For an analysis of this view, see Scott Kretchmar, "Ethics and Sport: An Overview," *Journal of the Philosophy of Sport*, 10 (1983), 21-32.

3. The formalist and reductionist positions have been expounded by such scholars as, Warren Fraleigh, *Right Action in Sports* (Champaign: Human Kinetics, 1984); Bernard Suits, *The Grasshopper: Games Life and Utopia* (Toronto: University of Toronto Press, 1978); and William J. Morgan, "The Logical Incompatibility Thesis and Rules: A Reconsideration of Formalism as an Account of Games," *Journal of the Philosophy of Sport,* 14 (1987), 1-19. For a critique of the formalistic approach see, Fred D'Agostino, "The Ethos of Games," *Journal of the Philosophy of Sport,* 8 (1981), 7-18.

4. For example, see Sondra Fraleigh, *Dance and the Lived Body: A Descriptive Aesthetic* (Pittsburgh: University of Pittsburgh Press, 1987).

5. For example, contrast Robert Simon's *Sport and Social Values* (Englewood Cliffs, NJ: Prentice-Hall, 1985), and almost any work by Scott Kretchmar, with George Leonard's *The Ultimate Athlete* (New York: Viking Press, 1975), and Michael Novak's *The Joy of Sport; End Zones, Bases, Baskets, Balls, and the Consecration of the American Spirit* (New York: Basic Books, 1976). The first pair represent the tendency to be Philosophical, in the sense in which Richard Rorty uses the term, and the second pair lean heavily toward being mystical. However, they are all essentially concerned with the play of sport and athletics, but make the mistake of trying to form a separate world of play/sport. As Drew Hyland has observed, they are dealing with play but they are not playful.

6. Culture criticism, as I use the term in this study, refers to a particular genre of reflective and analytical thought dealing with all aspects of our contemporary culture. The practitioners of this genre include, among

others, Michael Harrington, Noam Chomsky, Christopher Lasch, and to an extent, Richard Rorty.

7. Alasdair MacIntyre, *After Virtue: A Study in Moral Theory* (Notre Dame, IN: University of Notre Dame Press, 1984).

8. These various open positions are described in the following works; Drew Hyland, *The Question of Play* (Lanham, MD.: University Press of America, 1984); Alexander Nehamas, *Nietzsche: Life as Litertaure* (Cambridge, Mass: Harvard University Press, 1985); Richard Rorty, *The Consequences of Pragmatism* (Minneapolis: University of Minnesota Press, 1982).

9. James Keating, "Athletics and the Pursuit of Excellence" *Education*, 85 (1965), 428.

Chapter 1

1. Michael Harrington, *The Politics at God's Funeral, The Spiritual Crisis of Western Civilization* (New York: Viking Penguin, 1983), 74.

2. Alasdair MacIntyre, *After Virtue: A Study in Moral Theory* (Notre Dame, IN: University of Notre Dame Press, 1984), 117-118.

3. Nietzsche gives a powerful account of the cost of Ancient Greek society in *The Birth of Tragedy* (New York: Doubleday, 1956). He describes Hellenic Greece as the Apollonian triumph over the Dionysian, the triumph of the rational over the irrational. The result Nietzsche claims is Greek tragedy, and the root of the tragedy is the psychic cost of the suppression of the Dionysic.

4. The demise of Ancient Athens has been equated with the increasing individualism of citizenry. The citizen soldier came to be replaced by the professional soldier, and the wide spread participation in athletics gave way to spectatorship at events showcasing professional athletes. The increasing importance of the individuals freedom and declining requirements placed upon the citizen, together with the extension of citizenship to more individuals, went hand in hand with a reduction in the political significance of each individual citizen. For an account of these developments and their effects, see Deobald Van Dalen & Bruce L. Bennett, *A World History of Physical Education* (Englewood Cliffs, NJ: Prentice-Hall, 1971), 59-62. The situation in contemporary society seems to be similar, as a result of the Enlightenment's liberating effects we are free but lost in a world where the individual has become an autonomous but anchorless speck in a mass society.

5. Harrington, *The Politics at God's Funeral,* 12.

6. Stephen Toulmin, *Cosmoplis: The Hidden Agenda of Modernity,* (New York: The Free Press, 1990), 30-36.

7. Ibid., 82 and 128.

8. Ibid., 42.

9. Although Francis Bacon is quite rightly associated with the early development of scientific method for his work in pioneering inductive reasoning, Rene Descartes was responsible for putting the reasoning power of the individual at the center of scientific research. Bacon was essentially an empiricist, while Descartes based his method on the power of reason as the source of knowledge. Descartes built a whole philosophical system based on his method; in effect, he based his physics on a metaphysics. Bacon was more interested in the practical issues of knowledge and the potential it provided for man to conquer nature through the inductive discovery of the laws of nature. Descartes also had a greater grasp of the significance of mathematics than Bacon, for whom math represented an abstraction from the real world, that is, empirical world.

10. Harrington, *The Politics at Gold's Funeral, 30.* Harrington observes that when the Enlightenment replaced the old values with reason, truth became merely instrumental. What had started in the Enlightenment as the overthrow of the religious base of political power led to a situation where understanding is equated with control and dominance. We live in this Baconian world where knowledge is indeed power but one in which it is also reductionist and manipulative.

11. Ibid., 72.

12. Ibid., 73.

13. William Saler, "A Contextual Approach to an Understanding of Competition," in, Robert Ousterhoudt, (ed.), *The Philosophy of Sport; A Collection of Original Essays* (Springfield, Ill,: Charles C. Thomas, 1973), 180.

14. Ibid., 183.

15. Ibid.

16. Warren I. Susman, *Culture as History: The Transformation of American Society in the Twentieth Century* (New York: Pantheon, 1984), 273.

17. Ibid., 274.

18. Ibid.

19. Ibid., 276.

20. Ibid., 277.

21. Ibid., 276.

22. Ibid., 282.

23. Christopher Lasch, *The Culture of Narcissim: American Life in An Age of Diminishing Expectations* (New York: Warner, 1979).

24. Ibid., 21.

25. Ibid., 33.

26. Ibid., 43.

27. Ibid., 65.

28. Ibid., 139.

29. Ibid., 24.

30. Ibid., 25.

31. Ibid., 96.

32. Ibid., 114-15.

33. Ibid., 96-97.

34. Ibid., 98

35. MacIntyre, *After Virture,* 52.

36. Ibid., 32.

37. *North Dallas Forty,* MGM Movie, 1974.

38. MacIntyre, *After Virture,* 29.

39. Ibid.

40. Ibid., 26.

Chapter 2

1. Allan Guttmann, *From Ritual to Record: The Nature of Modern Sports* (New York: Columbia University Press, 1978).

2. For an analysis of "traditional" and "modern" ideal societal types see, Richard D. Brown, *Modernization: The Transformation of American Life, 1600-1865* (New York: Hill & Wang, 1976), 7-22. For a discussion of the importance of the impact of rationality on the development of modern sport see, Melvin L. Adelman, *A Sporting Time: New York and the Rise of Modern Athletics, 1820-70* (Urbana: University of Illinois Press, 1986), 5-10. Although rationality was evolving into the single most important concept in the Western world, there deloped serious and thoughtful conceptions that denied the authority of reason. These views did not consist in simple illogical or faulty thinking, but grew out of a rejection of the ambitious claims being made on the behalf of rationality, and the concomitant belief that the whole of existence has a comprehensible underpinning that is

knowable and predictable through the use of reason in the form of scientific method. This philosophical background fired a lineage of thinkers who questioned the justifiable jurisdiction of the powers of reason: Pascal, Schopenhauer, Sartre, Camus, Kierkegaard and Nietzsche, to name but a few. These men not only raised issues of epistemological, ontological, and ethical rationalism but also laid the ground for psychological and social irrationalist ideas that question the very rationality of the individual. The works of Freud, Jung, and Laing have all examined the issue of our rationality in human action and have raised important questions. These include the consideration of the individual's own understanding of his behavior. He may believe he is acting rationaly when really he is not. The power of prejudice, superstition, myths, pride, and the human adeptness at rationalization of behavior all fire and mask irrationality. Therefore, to deduce that we are rational beings because instrumental reason dominates our culture is erroneous. Rationality links means to ends, but rationality cannot choose the ends, and in this choice man is essentially irrational.

3. Melvin L. Adelman, "The First Modern Sport in America: Harness Racing In New York City, 1825-1870." *Journal of Sport History,* 8 (1981), 5.

4. Guttman, *From Ritual to Record,* 16: Adelman, "The First Modern Sport in America," 5-7.

5. For a discussion of sport as a natural religion see, Michael Novac, *The Joy of Sport* (New York: Basic, 1976), 18-34. For an account of the consequences of trying to elevate sport to the level of a natural religion see, Christopher Lasch, *The Culture of Narcissism* (New York: Warner, 1979), 181-220.

6. Guttman, *From Ritual to Record,* 26.

7. Donald J. Mrozek, *Sport and American Mentality 1880-1910* (Knoxville: University of Tennessee Press, 1983), 11.

8. For a discussion of the impact of the theoretical concept of equality on American political thought see Louis Haitz, *The Liberal Tradition in America: An Interpretation of American Political Thought Since the Revolution* (New York: Harcourt, Brace and World, 1955). For an analysis of the significance of hunting and social standing in medieval England see Thomas S. Henricks, "Sport and Social Hierarchy in Medieval England, "*Journal of Sport History,* 9 (1982).

9. For discussion of this issue see Richard S. Gruneau, "Class or Mass: Notes on the Democratization of Canadian Amateur Sport," in Richard S. Graneau and John G. Albinson, (ed), *Canadian Sport Sociology and Perspectives* (Don Mille, Ont.: Adison Wesley, 1976), and Harry Edwards, *The Sociology of Sport* (Homewood, Ill.: Dorsey Press, 1973).

10. Guttman, *From Ritual to Record,* 55.

11. Adelman, *A Sporting Time,* 29.

12. In the ten years from 1950-1960, the number of American homes with televisions rose from less that 10% to 94%. During that period television companies came increasingly to use sport to fill the slack weekend viewing periods on Saturday and Sunday afternoons. By the 1970s, the television audience for a weekend NFL games was over 20 million. The ability of televised sport to attract huge audiences resulted in increased packaging and promoting of the events. The television companies and advertising executives combined to produce a wildly accelerated commodification of sport. The power of television-money in sport makes the television companies automatic partners in any successful sporting enterprise, and their absence virtually assures financial collapse.

13. Although there is no causal link between modernization and commodification, it could be claimed that commodification is one of the many possible cultural manifestations of modernization. The link may seem a commonplace one, but it is not a necessary one.

14. Plato, *Republic Book III,* 404D, wrote athletics and gymnastics into his scheme of things and thus gave sport at least a marginal role in education, but he did not address the nature of sport itself and took its value as purely instrumental. Marx had even less to say about sport than Plato did, and Marxist sport philosophy is even more of an extrapolation than Platonist sport philosophy. Both genres have produced two basic positions: Plato is either interpreted as a dualist who saw the body as inherently inferior to the mind, or as educator who encouraged and valued physical activity, being a wrestler himself. Marx has been interpreted on one hand as rejecting the world of sport as trivial at best and dehumanizing and restrictive at worst. On the other hand, Marx is seen as recognizing all forms of human activity as potential unalienated *praxis.* The problem is that both Plato and Marx had their sights set beyond the realm of sport, Plato on the next world, and Marx on a free world, and the nature of sport was not an issue for either of them. At least Marx was concerned with this world, and sport represents a field of capitalist exploitation, and as such his views are relevant in an analysis of contemporary sport.

15. William S. Sahakian, *History of Philosophy* (New York: Barnes & Noble, 1968), 246.

16. Ibid., 247.

17. James Riordan, "Marx, Lenin, and Physical Culture," *Journal of Sport History,* 3 (summer 1976), 152.

18. Karl Marx, *A Contribution to the Critique of Political Economy* (Boston: Beacon Press, 1904), 12.

19. Karl Marx, "Economic and Philosophical Manuscripts of 1844," *Early Writings* (New York: Vintage, 1975), 360-61.

20. Riordan, "Marx, Lenin, and Physical Culture," 153.

21 Ibid.

22. For further discussion of these and related issues see John M. Hoberman, *Sport and Political Ideology* (Austin: University of Texas Press, 1984), 28-37.

23. Ibid.

24. Christopher Lasch, "The Degradation of Work and the Apotheosis of Art," *Harper's* (February 1984), 40-45.

25. Hoberman, *Sport and Political Ideology*, 35.

26. Ibid., 218.

27. Guttman, *From Ritual to Record,* 64.

28. Hoberman, *Sport and Political Ideology,* 222.

29. Ibid., 223.

30. Ibid., 225.

31. Ibid., 239.

32. Ibid., 240.

33. Ibid., 35.

34. Herbert Marcuse, *Eros and Civilization* (New York: Vintage, 1961), xi.

35. Guttman, *From Ritual to Record,* 66.

36. Ibid.

37. Theodor W. Adorno, *Prisms* (london: Neville Spearman, 1967), 81.

38. Roland Barthes, *The Eiffel Tower and Other Mythologies* (New York: Hill & Wang, 1979), 87-88.

39. James Riordan, *Sport in Soviet Society* (Cambridge: Cambridge University Press, 1977), 59-60.

40. Hoberman, *Sport and Political Ideology,* 192.

41. Allan Guttmann, *Sports Spectators* (New York: Columbia University Press, 1986), 184.

42. Friedrich Nietzsche, *Beyond Good and Evil* (Harmondsworth: Penguin, 1973), 146.

43. Christopher Lasch, *The Culture of Narcissism: American Life in an Age of Diminished Expectations* (New York: Warner, 1979), 22-26.

44. John J. Sewart, "The Rationalization of Modern Sport: The Case of Professional Football," *Arena,* 1 (fall 1975), 46.

45. Ibid.

46. Benjamin G. Radar, *American Sports: From the Age of Folk Games to the Age of Spectators* (Englewood Cliffs, NJ: Prentice-Hall, 1983), v.

47. Steven A. Riess, *Touching Base: Professional Baseball and American Culture in the Progressive Era* (Westport, CN: Greenwood Press, 1980), 153: and Rader, *American Sports,* 114.

48. Rader, *American Sports,* 115.

49. Ibid.

50. Harold Seymour, *Baseball: The Early Years* (New York: Oxford University Press, 1960), 110.

51. Rader, *American Sports,* 209.

52. Cable News Network, broadcast interview (March 15, 1987).

53. Sewart, "Rationalization," 49.

54. Ibid., 50.

55. Ray Kennedy & Nancy Williamson, "Money, The Monster Threatening Modern Sports," *Sports Illustrated* (July 17, 1973), 35-38, 54-57, 71-72.

56. Michael Oriard, "Professional Football as Cultural Myth," *Journal of American Culture,* 5 (1980), 29.

57. Sewart, "Rationalization," 48.

58. Ibid.

59. For discussion of sport as myth see Michael Novak, *The Joy of Sports: End Zones, Bases, Baskets, Balls and the Consecration of the American Spirit* (New York: Basic Books, 1976), 56-115.

60. Oriard, "Professional Football," 40.

61. Lasch, *The Culture of Narcissism,* 185.

62. Johan Huizinga, *Homo Ludens: A study of the Play Element in Culture* (Boston: Beacon Hill Press, 1955), 48.

63. Ibid., 197-98.

64. Lasch, *The Culture of Narcissism,* 188.

65. Ibid., 190.

66. Ibid., 192.

67. Ibid., 195.

68. Novak, *The Joy of Sports,* 248-69.

69. Lasch, *The Culture of Narcissism,* 216.

Chapter 3

1. James Keating, "Athletics and the purist of excellence." *Education,* 85 (1965), 428.

2. Ibid., 429.

3. Ibid.

4. Ibid.

5. Ibid., 430.

6. Ibid.

7. Ibid., 431.

8. Etienne Gilson, in Anton Pegis (ed.), *A Gilson Reader* (Garden City, NJ: Doubleday Image Books, 1957), 323.

9. James Keating, "Winning in Sport and Athletics." *Thought,* 38 (summer 1963), 202.

10. Ibid.

11. Forest Evashcvski, *Sports Illustrated* (Sept. 23, 1957), 119.

12. Earl Blaik, *You Have to Pay the Price* (New York: Holt. Rhinchart & Winston, 1960), 313.

13. Woody Hayes, *Sports Illustrated,* (Sept. 24, 1962), 135.

14. Keating, "Winning in Sport and Athletics," 203.

15. Ibid.

16. Ibid., 204.

17. Ibid.

18. The simple jargon of sport philosophy expressed in terms like play, games, sport, athletics, contest, competition, winning, athlete, sportsman, player, and so on, have been discussed at some length in the literature that makes up that genre called sport philosophy. But no definitive positions have been universally established for these terms. The language analysis approach to philosophy as a whole is seen as a barren enterprise by many

pragmatic and existential philosophers; see Richard Rorty, *Philosophy and the Mirror of Nature* (Princeton, N.J.: Princeton University Press, 1980) for an extended analysis of this area. While I would agree that we will not find and ultimate truth or the true nature of play, games, etc. from a language analysis study, we can use it to help clarify our positions, to make it clear what we are talking about. As such, the discussions of the meanings of the common vocabulary of sport philosophy is valid as a starting point for clarification, but hardly as an end in itself.

19. Play has been the subject of the reflections and analysis of philosophers from the pre-Socratics to the present day. Heraclitus (Fragment 52) saw the playing child moving pieces in a game as a model of human existence. Plato (*Symposium* 276d) took philosophy to be the play of the wise, and Schiller (*On The Aesthetic Education of Man* {New York: Ungar, 1965}, 80.) thought us to be our most human in play. This philosophical interest in play blossomed along with academia itself into psychological, sociological, historical, medical, and financial studies of play. Play was the earliest recipient of academic study in the development of what I have called the vocabulary of sport philosophy, and not games, sport or any of the other terms.

20. Roger Caillois, *Man, Play and Games* (New York: Free Press, 1961). 9-10.

21. Carolyn Thomas, *Sport in a Philosophic Context* (Philadelphia: Lea and Febiger, 1983) 58-72.

22. Gregory Bateson, "A Theory of Play and Fantasy" in Janet Harris & Roberta Park (ed.), *Play Games and Sport in Cultural Context* (Champaign, III.: Human Kinetics Press, 1983), 315.

23. John Loy, "The Nature of Sports," in Harris & Park (ed.) *Play Games and Sport,* 44.

24. Allan Guttmann, *From Ritual to Records: The Nature of Modern Sports* (New York: Columbia University Press, 1978), 4.

25. Ibid., 6.

26. Harold Vanderzwaag, *Towards a Philosophy of Sport* (Reading, Mass.: Addison Wesley, 1972), 72.

27. Drew Hyland, *The Question of Play* (Lanham, MD: University Press of America, 1984), 123.

28. Alasdair MacIntyre, *After Virtue: A Study in Moral Theory* (Notre Dame, IN: University of Notre Dame Press, 1981), 137.

29. Klaus Meier, "An Affair of Flutes; An Appreciation of Play," *Journal of the Philosophy of Sport,* 7 (fall 1980), 31.

30. Hyland, *The Question of Play,* 47.

31. Ibid., 148.

32. Plato, *Symposium,* 189c-193d.

33. Ibid.

34. Hyland, *The Question of Play,* 141-42.

35. Ibid., 143.

36. Ibid., 144.

37. Ibid.

38. Ibid.

39. G. Alan Stull & Guy M. Lewis, "The Funeral Games of the Homeric Greeks," *Quest,* 11 (1968) 4. For other works supporting this position see; Werner Jaeger, *Paideia: The Ideals of Greek Culture I* (Oxford: Blackwell, 1939), 5; Harold Kitto, *The Greeks* (Baltimore, MD: Penguin, 1960), 240; and H.Z. Marrose, *A History of Education in Antiquity* (New York: New American Library, 1964), 32.

40. Matthew W. Dickie, "Fair and Foul Play in the Funeral Games in the Illiad." *Journal of Sport History,* 11 (summer 1984), 17. See also, Clarence Forbes, *Greek Physical Education* (New York: The Century Co., 1929).

41. MacIntyre, *After Virtue,* 128.

42. Christopher Lasch, *The Culture of Narcissism: American Life in an Age of Diminishing Expectations* (New York: Warner, 1979).

43. Keating, "Athletics and the Pursuit of Excellence," 431.

44. Gilson, *A Gilson Reader,* 323.

45. Keating, "Sport and Athletics," 203.

Chapter 4

1. Michael Harrington, *The Politics ar God's Funeral: The Spiritual Crisis of Western Civilization* (New York: Viking Penguin, 1983), 94.

2. Friedrich Nietzsche, *The Birth of Tragedy* (Garden City, NY: Doubleday, 1956), 145.

3. Ibid., 146.

4. Ibid., 92.

5. Ibid.

6. Ibid., 93.

7. Ibid.

8. In the *Apology* (38d-41a) Socrates explains the irrationality of fearing death, yet his rationality does not admit the basis of much human fear; fear of the unknown. Socrates does not claim to know what happens at death, but he does hold that there is no rational basis to fear death at all. To Nietzsche the symbol of the rational Socrates facing death in so calculating a manner is an icon to all rational inquiry. Yet today we fear the unknown, the unexplainable, and things that cannot be controlled through our intellectual dominance of them through data and theory. These areas are either discounted or discredited as the realm of madcaps and fools, or avoided and culturally suppressed. But it is just this frontier of scientific knowledge where the communicative and explicative values of art and literature become more important.

9. Nietzsche, *The Birth of Tragedy,* 93.

10. Friedrich Nietzsche, *The Gay Science* (New York: Vintage Books, 1974), 296.

11. The Nietzschean answer to the Socratic icon to science, the rational man facing death without fear based on his rational assessment of the available data, is the existential tragic hero, the 'overman'. Nietzsche shows us a character who faces the horrors of life and death with a strength born of his own weakness, a hope drawn from the hopelessness of the human condition, a pool of order created by the will of the man from the chaos of existence. What Nietzsche cannot forgive in Socrates is his pretense that there is order, although we might not see it clearly at this moment. The Socratic icon deludes us and offers the hope of objectivity and rationality. Nietzsche faces the maelstrom and gives subjectivity and irrationality because ultimately that is all that there is.

12. Nietzsche, *The Gay Science,* 331.

13. To Nietzsche this distinction was very important, and holds a significant insight to post-Enlightenment life. The opposition of good and evil represents the clash of absolutes, but when good and bad are compared the tone is less shrill, and is certainly less of an appeal to metaphysics than to pragmatics.

14. Alexander Nehamas, *Nietzsche: Life as Literature* (Cambridge, Mass.: Harvard University Press, 1985), 1-5.

15. Ibid.

16. Nietzsche, *The Anti-Christ* (Harmondsworth: Penguin, 1972), 173.

17. Nietzsche, *The Gay Science,* 338.

18. Alasdair MacIntyre, *After Virtue: A Study In Moral Theory* (Notre Dame, IN: University of Notre Dame Press, 1984), 113.

19. Richard J. Bernstein, *Philosophical Profiles* (Philadelphia: University of Pennsylvania Press, 1986), 118.

20. MacIntyre, *After Virtue,* 117.

21. Ibid., 256.

22. Ibid., 257-259.

23. Ibid., 184.

24. Ibid., 185.

25. Ibid., 186.

26. Ibid., 187.

27. Ibid.

28. Ibid., 189.

29. Ibid., 190.

30. Ibid., 191.

31. Ibid.

32. Ibid., 193.

33. Ibid., 194.

34. Bernstein, *Philosophical Profiles,* 123-124.

35. Ibid., 125.

36. MacIntyre, *After Virtue,* 196.

37. Ibid., 193.

38. Ibid., 201.

39. Ibid., 202.

40. Ibid., 204.

41. Ibid., 205.

42. Ibid., 206.

43. Ibid., 208.

44. Ibid., 219.

45. Ibid.

46. Bernstein, *Philosophical Profiles,* 127.

47. MacIntyre, *After Virtue,* 183.

48. Bernstein, *Philosophical Profiles,* 131.

49. MacIntyre, *After Virtue,* 223.

50. Bernstein, *Philosophical Profiles,* 133.

51. Ibid., 134.

52. Ibid.

53. Ibid., 135-36.

54. Ibid., 139.

Chapter 5

1. In this study post-modern philosophy should be understood as the deconstructive trend that developed as a response to the scientific optimism of modernity. The post-modern philosophy seeks an escape from epistemology, but resists the temptation to replace it with anything else. The idea that we can ever know in any final sense is rejected, because meaning and knowledge are not out there but within our interpretation. As Nietzsche said, there is no meaning, only interpretation. This genre of philosophy arguably dating from Nietzsche, and less arguably from Wittenstein, Heidegger and Dewey, has given free reign to the likes of Habermas, Gadamer, Derrida, Foucault and Rorty. My understanding of post-modern philosophy is most influenced by Rorty, Habermas, and Foucault.

2. Richard Bernstein, *Philosophical Profiles* (Philadelphia: University of Pennsylvania Press, 1986), 60.

3. Richard Rorty, *Consequences of Pragmatism* (Minneapolis: University of Minnesota Press, 1982), xiv.

4. Ibid., xii.

5. Jurgen Habermas, *Knowledge and Human Interests* (Boston: Beacon Press, 1971), 208.

6. Bernstein, *Philosophical Profiles,* 78.

7. Rorty, *Consequences of Pragmatism,* xliii.

8. Ibid., 166.

9. Ibid., 165.

10. Ibid., 208.

11. The idea that *phroneses* makes the technician of a craftsman is developed by Hans-Georg Gadamer, "The problem of Historical Consciousness," in P. Rabinow & W. M. Sullivan (ed), *Interpretive Social Science: A Reader* (Berkeley: University of California Press, 1979), 113.

12. Bernstein, *Philosophical Profiles,* 88.

13. Rorty, *Consequences of Pragmatism,* 164.

14. Ibid., 172.

15. Rorty, The 1986 Northcliffe Lectures, III, "The Contingency of Community."

16. *Razor's Edge,* MGM Movie, 1984.

Chapter 6

1. Gary Smith, "Tyson the Timid, Tyson the Terrible," *Sports Illustrated,* 68 (March 21, 1988), 75.

2. Friedrich Nietzsche, *The Twilight of the Idols* (Harmondsworth: Penguin, 1968), 23.

3. *North Dallas Forty,* Paramount Movie, 1969.

4. *Apocalypse Now,* MGM Movie, 1973.

5, Gary Stevens, "Soccer and Politics," *Soccer America* (April 15, 1988), 15.

6. Richard Rorty, The 1986 Northcliffe Lectures, III, "The Contingency of Community."

7. Richard Rorty, *The Consequences of Pragmatism* (Minneapolis: University of Minnesota Press, 1982), 208.

8. Jergen Habermas, "Neo-Conservative Culture Criticism in the United States and West Germany: An Intellectual Movement in Two Political Cultures," in Richard Bernstein (ed.) *Habermas and Modernity* (Cambridge: The MIT Press, 1985), 81.

9. Ibid., 83.

10. Ibid., 93.

11. Bernstein, *Habermas and Modernity,* 7.

12. Friedrich Nietzsche, *The Gay Science* (New York: Vintage, 1974), 219.

13. Smith, "Tyson the Timid, Tyson the Terrible," 76.

14. Ibid., 84.

15. Jergen Habermas, "A Reply to My Critics", in John S. Thompson & David Heid, (ed.), Habermas : Critical Debate (London: Penguin, 1982), 227.

16. Smith, "Tyson the Timid, Tyson the Terrible," 80.

17. Ibid., 82.

18. Seymour Kleinman, "Art, Sport and Intention," NAPEHE Proceedings, Vol. I, (Champaign, ILL: Human Kinetics, 1980), 219.

19. Ibid.

20. David Best, "The Aesthetic in Sport," in Ellen Gerber and William Morgan (ed.) *Sport and the Body,* 2nd Edition (Philadelphia: Lea & Febiger, 1979).

21. David Best, "Sport is Not Art," *Journal of the Philosophy of Sport,* 11 (1985), 30.

22. Rorty, *The Consequences of Pragmatism,* 172.

23. Seymour Kleiman, "The Athlete as Performing Artist: The Embodiment of Sport Literature and Philosophy," Paper Presented at the Sport Literature Association Conference, San Diego, California, July 27, 1984, 4.

24. Laurie McMenamy, quoted in Desmond Morris, *The Soccer Tribe* (London: Jonathon Cape 1981), 126.

25. Allan Bloom, *The Closing of the American Mind, How Higher Education Has Failed Democracy and Impoverished the Souls of Today's Students* (New York: Simon and Schuster, 1987), 74.

26. Christopher Lasch, "The Apotiosis of Art and the Degredation of Work," *Harpers* (Feb. 1984), 44.

27. The International Surfing Association; The European Surfing Association; and the World Flying Disc Federation; Examples of a world dedicated to international unification of rules and the staging of world championships. Karen E. Koen (ed.), *Encyclopedia of Associations,* vol. 4, International Organizations, (Detroit: Book Tower, 1988), 547, 547 & 538, respectively.

28. *North Dallas Forty,* Paramount Movie, 1969.

29. It should be pointed out at this point that the expressions, "effortless effort," "artless art," and "letting the game play you" all have their roots in

eastern philosophy. While I have a deep personal and scholarly interest in eastern philosophy, especially Zen Buddhism and Taoism, and have been greatly influenced by these venerable bodies of knowledge, it is not my wish to introduce them to this study. I feel it is more appropriate for this study to work out of western intellectual tradition. Robert Persig's brilliant book, *Zen and the Art of Motorcycle Maintenance* (New York : Morrow Quill, 1979), bridges the gap between eastern and western thought to a large extent, and was also a major influence in the early formulation of the questions and answers contained in my study.

30. Bloom, *The Closing of the American Mind,* 42

Conclusion

1. Friedrich Nietzsche, *The Wanderer and His Shadow,* 251, in R.J. Holingdale (ed.), *A Nietzsche Reader* (Harmondsworth: Penguin, 1984), 278.

2. Alasdair MacIntyre, *After Virtue: A Study in Moral Theory* (Notre Dame, IN: University of Notre Dame Press, 1984), 263.

3. Jacob Bronowski, *The Ascent of Man* (Boston: Little, Brown & Co., 1973), 438.

4. Alexander Nehamas, *Nietzsche: Life as Literature* (Cambridge, Mass.: Harvard University Press, 1985).

5. Richard Rorty, *The Consequences of Pragmatism* (Minneapolis: University Press, 1983), xliv.

Bibliography

Adelman, Melvin L. "The First Modern Sport in America; Harness Racing in New York City, 1825-1870." *Journal of Sport History,* vol. 8, No. 1 (spring 1981).

———.*A Sporting Time: New York City and Rise of Modern Athletics, 1820-70.* Urbana: University of Illinois Press, 1986.

Adorno, Theodore. *Prisms.* London: Neville Spearman, 1967.

———. *Introduction to the Sociology of Music.* New York : Saebury Press, 1976.

Barthes, Roland. *The Eiffel Tower and Other Mythologies.* New York: Hill & Wang, 1979.

Bateson, Gregory. "A theory of Play and Fantasy." In Harris, Carolyn, & Parks, Roberta, (ed.). *Play, Games and Sports in a Cultural Context.* Champaine, Illinois: Human Kinetics Press, 1983.

Beisser, Arnold. *The Madness in Sport.* Bowie, Maryland: Charles Press, 1977.

Bell, David. *The Cultural Contradictions of Capitalism.* New York : Basic Books, 1976.

Berman, Marshall. *All That is Solid Melts Into Air: The Experience of Modernity.* New York: Viking Penguin, 1982.

Bernstein, Richard. *Beyond Objectivism and Realism: Science, Hermeneutics, and Praxis.* Philadelphia: University of Pennsylvania Press, 1985.

———. *Philosophical Profiles; Essays in a Pragmatic Mode.* Philadelphia: University of Pennsylvania Press, 1986.

———. (ed.). *Habermas and Modernity.* Cambridge: MIT Press, 1985.

Best, David. "The Aesthetic in Sport." In Gerber, Ellen & Morgan, William, (ed.) *Sport and the Body.* 2nd edition, Philadelphia: Lea & Febiger, 1979.

————. "Sport is Not Art." *Journal of the Philosophy of Sport,* vol. 12, 1985.

Bloom, Allan. *The Closing of the American Mind. How Higher Education Has Failed Democracy and Impoverished the Souls of Today's Students.* New York: Simon & Schuster, 1987.

Bromowski, Jacob. *The Ascent of Man.* Boston: Little Brown & Co., 1973.

Caillois, Roger. *Man, Play and Games.* New York: Free Press of Glencoe, 1961.

Carse, James P. *Finite and Infinite Games: A Vision of Life as Play and Possibility.* New York: Free Press, 1986.   ▪

Dickie, Matthew W. "Fair and Foul Play in the Funeral Games in the Illiad." *Journal of Sport History.* 11 (summer 1984).

Gent, Peter, *North Dallas Forty.* New York: Morrow, 1973.

Guttman, Allan. *From Ritual to Record: The Nature of Modern Sports.* New York: Columbia University Press, 1978.

————. *Sports Spectators.* New York: Columbia University Press, 1986.

————. *A Whole New Ball Game: An Interpretation of American Sports.* Chapel Hill, North Carolina: University of North Carolina Press, 1988.

Habermas, Jurgen. *Knowledge and Human Interests.* Boston: Beacon Hill Press, 1971.

————. *The Theory of Communicative Action, Volume 1; Reason and the Rationalization of Society.* Boston: Beacon Press, 1981.

————. "Neo-Conservative Culture Criticism in the United States and West Germany: An Intellectual Movement in Two Political Cultures." In Bernstein, Richard, (ed.). *Habermas and Modernity.* Cambridge: MIT Press, 1985.

Harrington, Michael. *The Politics at God's Funeral: The Spiritual Crisis of Western Civilization.* New York: Viking Penguin, 1983.

Hoberman, John. *Sport and Political Ideology.* Austin: University of Texas Press, 1984.

Hollinger, Robert (ed.). *Hermeneutics and Praxis.* Notre Dame: University of Notre Dame Press, 1985.

Huizinga, Johan. *Homo Ludens: A Study of the Play Element in Culture.* Boston: Beacon Hill Press, 1955.

Hyland, Drew. *The Question of Play.* Lanham, MD: University Press of America, 1984.

Keating, James. "Athletics and the Persuit of Excellence." *Education,* 85 (March 1965).

————. Winning in Sport and Athletics." *Thought,* 38 (summer 1963).

Kennedy, Ray, & Williamson, Nancy. "Money, the Monster Threatening Modern Sports." *Sports Illustrated* (July 17, 1978).

Kleinman, Seymour, (ed.). *Mind and Body: East Meets West.* Champaign, Ill.: Human Kinetics, 1986.

———. "Art, Sport and Intention." NAPEHE Proceedings, vol.I, Champaign, Ill.: Human Kinetics, 1980.

———. "The Athlete as Performing Artist: The Emodiment of Sport Literature and Philosophy." Paper presented at the Sport Literature Association Conference, San Diego, California, July 27, 1984.

Lasch, Christopher. *The Culture of Narcissism: American Life in an Age of Diminishing Expectations.* New York: Warner, 1979.

———. "The Degradation of Work and the Apotheosis of Art." *Harper's* (February 1984).

Leonard, George. *The Ultimate Athlete.* New York: Viking 1975.

Lipsyte, Robert. *Sports World: An American Dreamland.* New York: Quadrangle, 1975.

Loy, John. "The Nature of Sports." In Harris, Carolyn, & Parks, Roberta, (ed.). *Play, Games and Sport In A Cultural Context.* Champaign, Ill.: Human Kinetics, 1983.

MacIntyre, Alasdair. *Whose Justice? Which Rationality?* Notre Dame, IN: University of Notre Dame Press, 1988.

———. *After Virtue: A Study in Moral Theory.* Notre Dame, IN: University of Notre Dame Press, 1984.

Marcuse, Herbert. *One Dimensional Man: Studies in the Ideology of Advanced Industrial Society.* Boston: Beacon Press, 1966.

———. *Eros and Civilization.* New York: Vintage, 1955.

Marx, Karl. *Early Writings.* New York: Vintage, 1975.

Meier, Klaus. "An Affair of Flutes: An Appreciation of Play." *Journal of the Philosophy of Sport,* 7 (fall 1980).

Mihalich, Joseph. *Sports and Athletics: Philosophy in Action.* Totowa, NJ: Littlefield, Adams & Co., 1982.

Morris, Desmond. *The Soccer Tribe.* London: Jonathon Cape, 1981.

Mrozek, Donald. *Sport and American Mentality 1880-1910.* Knoxville: University of Tennessee Press, 1983.

Nehamas, Alaxander, *Nietzsche: Life as Literature.* Cambridge, Mass: Harvard University Press, 1985.

Nietzsche, Friedrich. *The Gay Science.* New York: Vintage, 1974.

————. *The Birth of Tragedy & the Genealogy of Morals* New York: Doubleday, 1956.

————. *Beyond Good and Evil: Prelude to Philosophy of the Future.* Harmondsworth: Penguin, 1973.

————. *Twilight of the Idols & The Anti-Christ.* Harmondsworth: Penguin, 1968.

Novak, Michael. *The Joy of Sports: End Zones, Bases, Baskets, Balls and the Consecration of the American Spirit.* New York: Basic Books, 1976.

Oriard, Michael. "Professional Football as Cultural Myth." *Journal of American Culture,* 5.

Pirsig, Robert M. *Zen and the Art of Motorcycle Maintenance: An Inquiry Into Values.* New York: Morrow, 1979.

Plato. *Great Dialogues of Plato.* New York: Signet, 1956.

Rader, Benjamin G. *American Sports: From the Age of Folk Games to the Age of Spectators.* Englewood Cliffs, NJ: Prentice-Hall, 1983.

Riess, Steven A. *Touching Base: Professional Baseball and American Culture in the Progressive Era.* Westport, ON.: Greenwood Press, 1980.

Riordan, James. *Sport in Soviet Society.* Cambridge: Cambridge University Press, 1977.

————. "Marx, Lenin, and Physical Culture." *Journal of Sport History* 3 (summer 1976).

Rorty, Richard. *Philosophy and the Mirror of Nature.* Princeton: Princeton University Press, 1979.

————. *The Consequences of Pragmatism.* Minneapolis: University of Minnesota Press, 1982.

Sadler, William. "A Contextual Approach to an Understanding of Competition." In Ousterhoudt, Robert, *The Philosophy of Sport.* Springfield, Ill.: Thomas, 1973.

Seymour, Harold. *Baseball: The Early Years.* New York: Oxford University Press, 1960.

Sewart, John J. "The Rationalization of Modern Sport: The Case of Professional Football." *Arena,* 1 (fall 1975).

Simon, Robert L. *Sports and Social Values.* Englewood Cliffs, NJ: Prentice-Hall, 1985.

Smith, Gary. "Tyson the Timid, Tyson the Terrible." *Sports Illustrated* 68, 12 (March 21, 1988).

Smith, Philip L. *Sources of Progressive Thought in American Education.* Lanham, MD: University Press of America, 1980.

———. *The Problem of Values in Educational Thought.* Ames, Iowa: Iowa State University Press, 1982.

Soar, Phil, Tyler, Martin, and Widdows, Richard. *The Hamlyn Encyclopedia of Football.* London: Hamlyn, 1984.

Stull, G. Alan, and Lewis, Guy M. "The Funeral Games of the Homeric Greeks." *Quest* 11, 1968.

Susman, Warren I. *Culture as History: The Transformation of American Society in the Twentieth Century.* New York: Pantheon, 1984.

Taylor, Charles. *Sources of the Self: The Making of the Modern Identity.* Cambridge, MA: Harvard University Press, 1989.

Thomas, Carolyn. *Sport in a Philosophic Context.* Philadelphia: Lea & Febiger, 1983.

Toulmin, Stephen. *Cosmopolis: The Hidden Agenda of Modernity.* New York, NY: The Free Press, 1990.

Walzer, Michael. "The Politics of Michael Foucault." In Couzens Hoy, David (ed.), *Foucault: A Critical Reader.* Oxford: Basil Blackwell, 1986.

Index